Kites

Flying Skills and Techniques, from Basic Toys to Sport Kites

Rosanne Cobb

FIREFLY BOOKS

Published by Firefly Books Ltd. 2007
Copyright © 2007 Collins & Brown
Copyright text © 2007 Rosanne Cobb

First printing

Publisher Cataloging-in-Publication Data (U.S.)

Cobb, Rosanne.
Kites: flying skills and techniques, from basic toys to sport kites/Rosanne Cobb;
Richard Burgess.
[125] p. : col. photos. ;   cm.
Included bibliographical references and index.
Summary: Includes what kite to fly and buy, basic flying skills, understanding equipment and the wind; also covers the fundamentals of kite sports including kite boarding, kite surfing, kite bugging and snow kiting.
ISBN-13: 978-1-55407-262-0   (pbk.)
ISBN-10: 1-55407-262-X   (pbk.)
1. Kites. I. Burgess, Richard. II. Title.
629.133 /32 dc22   TL759.C633 2007

Library and Archives Canada Cataloguing in Publication

Cobb, Rosanne
    Kites : flying skills and techniques, from basic toys to sport kites / Rosanne
Cobb ; illustrations: Richard Burgess ; photographs: Janie Airey.

Includes bibliographical references and index.
ISBN-13: 978-1-55407-262-0
ISBN-10: 1-55407-262-X
    1. Kites. I. Burgess, Richard II. Airey, Janie III. Title.
TL759.C62 2007   796.15'8   C2006-905745-1

Published in the United States by
Firefly Books (U.S.) Inc.
P.O. Box 1338, Ellicott Station
Buffalo, New York 14205

Published in Canada by
Firefly Books Ltd.
66 Leek Crescent
Richmond Hill, Ontario L4B 1H1

Printed in China

Contents

Introduction

Kite flying is a pastime enjoyed by millions the world over, across all cultures and age ranges; from the Inuit to the Irish, the Tibetans to the Turkish, all can appreciate the joy of flying a kite high above them in the sky. Kite flying was invented over 3,000 years ago in Asia. The Chinese military used kites to spy on the enemy, to send messages and to lift themselves out of sticky situations. But it wasn't all work. With bamboo, rubber and silk, the inventive Chinese were able to create all types of playthings, including musical kites that emitted sounds when blowing on the wind. Once the Chinese artistic flair was applied to their creations, it is not surprising that kites became items to be worshiped and to which great superstition was often attached.

The popularity of kites quickly spread to neighboring countries. So many people were flying kites instead of working in Japan in the 18th century that the government banned the pastime, as there was a detrimental effect on the working day. Children in Afghanistan and Thailand were staging whole-day events flying kites with fiercely sharp lines in order to ruthlessly bring down other kites in the sky.

Indonesians used the leaves from trees to create kites they used for fishing (and still do!).

Some time later the Western world caught the bug for flying. Predictably, kites were used in the late 19th century in warfare, and in World War II they were used as target practice. However, a greater use for kites was found in the realms of science and transportation. Due to their ability to reach places that other instruments cannot reach, kites have helped advance our understanding of the atmosphere. (Were it not for kites we would have taken a long time to understand the effects of altitude on temperature, or the electrical nature of lightning, for example.) Without kites as forerunners – and the inventive thinking of the Wright brothers – it is unlikely we would be so adept at air travel. Samuel Franklin Cody almost succeeded in crossing the English Channel in 1903 in a boat powered by two kites.

Kiting has enjoyed a surge of popularity in the past 50 years for two reasons. First, kites have ceased to be of such importance in warfare or transportation as more sophisticated methods of research and travel have been developed. This has meant that kites have been redefined as playthings once again. Second, material and design capabilities have advanced considerably. The development of ripstop nylon, fiberglass and the various compounds of other new materials has allowed the limitless development of kites, and the sports associated with them.

The variety of kites flown today is as broad as the sky is vast. Single-line kites are great fun to watch in the air and are still the main attraction at the numerous kite festivals around the world.

Single-line kites can be small and simple like the diamond kites of *Mary Poppins* fame, or elaborate and enormous air creations, some of which can total 10,000 ft. square (3,050 m square).

The main kite disciplines enjoying a growth in popularity, and two of the most exhilarating sports to explode in recent years, are stunt kiting and power kiting. Stunt kites (also called sport kites) are highly maneuverable two-line kites that can perform tricks and intricate dancing sequences in the air. Power kites (also called traction kites) are parachute-like kites that are used to generate lift and forward motion for the flier. Flying these huge, powerful kites, on land or water, on foot, in a buggy or on a board, is referred to as power kiting.

These two kite types occupy different spaces in the kiting world. Stunt kites, although not small, are about delicate maneuvers, purposeful stalling, reversing, looping and swooping. The joy of flying them is in being able to direct them to perform dancing maneuvers and create patterns in the sky. Although the pleasure in flying power kites also comes from perfecting control, the effect of that control has nothing to do with a pretty dancing kite. The big, slow power kite is used to create not a spectacle in the air, but an exhilarating spectacle at the level of the flier as he or she is pulled forward and upward. From its roots in recreational flying, power kiting has fast become an independent mainstream sport enjoyed by people from all walks of life.

Whether kites are big or small, homemade or factory-designed, flown for power or beauty, all are a truly inspiring spectacle and never less than fantastic fun to fly.

1 Understanding kites and equipment

Here you will learn how to distinguish between power kites and stunt kites as well as the more simple one-line kites that are ideal if you have never flown a kite before. Other equipment you may need is also explained and illustrated, allowing you to work out what you need to get started. One of the joys of kite flying is that it can be gloriously simple to get started, with a minimum of equipment or extra expense. Once you decide to try power kiting or a more specialized form of kite flying you may need to invest in some safety equipment.

Choosing your kite

The graceful bird of prey lends its name to the human-made kite because of their similar appearance as they soar in the sky. Just as there are more than 10,000 species of birds, each with their individual way of hovering, swooping and diving, there are literally thousands of kites in existence in a variety of shapes and sizes.

Traditional one-line diamond kites, or one-line parafoils, are the easiest kites to manage, with children as young as two or three years old able to successfully fly them, as well as make them! There are kites as small as leaves for those who don't like carrying equipment, and as big as a small tree for those who like to create a spectacle. You don't even need wind these days, as there are, incredibly, indoor kites.

Unfortunately, the kiting world has almost as many names as there are kites to describe this plethora of kite types, with blurred boundaries for what these names refer to. Each subsection of the kiting community has its own terminology with its own way of categorizing different kites. As it would take pages to describe all the kite types and their corresponding intricate relationships, this chapter gives only a general guide. Be aware that each kite-crazed community takes its craft very seriously, so expect severe reprisal should you choose to take lightly the distinction between them!

Although less than succinct, the various categories of kite types can be defined by both the number of lines on which they fly and their purpose. Using this system, there are three main categories of the most popular kite types.

Single-line decorative kites

These are mainly flown simply for the spectacle they create when hovering in the air, and include
▷ Flat kites (flat when in the air)
▷ Bowed (bowed when in the air)
▷ Figure (recognizable as objects such as birds or animals)
▷ Rokkaku (six-sided, tall and symmetrical)
▷ Cellular (rigid 3-D kites)
▷ Delta (triangular wing shape after the Greek letter *delta*; a more basic version of a stunt kite)
▷ Train (kites attached to one another)
▷ Fighter kites (maneuverable kites used for "fighting" to bring other kites out of the sky)

Stunt/sport kites

Stunt kites have two lines to control the kite and are designed for maximum maneuverability. Most stunt kites fall into the delta category as they have two triangular wings, as well as spars (skeletal poles that give the kite structure) on the leading edges holding their shape.

There are also four-line stunt kites that are shaped like a bow tie, but these are not so common. Generally, the terms "stunt kite" and "sport kite" are synonymous and almost always refer to these small rigid-framed two-line kites. However, be aware that some people refer to small power kites as stunt kites because of the ease with which stunts can be performed when the size of a power kite is reduced.

Multiline power/traction kites

These are two-, four- and five-line kites designed to harness the wind's power. The terms "power kite" and "traction kite" are usually used interchangeably and both refer to the fact that the kite can be harnessed to create power to pull an object. Just as in the general world of kites, the distinctions between kite types in the power kiting community are as sharp as clay. Power kites can be distinguished according to how many lines they have, whether they are made for land or water flying, or according to which sport they are designed for. The easiest way to understand power kites is by splitting them into two main categories:

▷ **Foils/land kites** (air filling the cells gives the kite shape). These kites are used for flying on land and may have two or four lines.
▷ **Inflatable/water-relaunchable** (inflatable bladders give the kite shape). These kites are used for flying on water.

Basic kite design

It is useful to understand some basics of kite design before choosing a kite to fly. The manufacturer will usually summarize the effect of each kite model's characteristics so that you don't have to know, for example, how a high aspect ratio affects the kite's flight, or the virtues of carbon versus fiberglass. However, the manufacturer will often oversimplify, with limited comments such as "suitable for beginners," so knowing a bit about the following variables will be invaluable when buying your own kite.

AR

Aspect ratio is the relationship between the length of the kite and its height, or, more specifically, it is the length of the wingspan divided by the length of the chord, which is an imaginary line drawn from the leading edge to the trailing edge of the kite. The higher the AR (i.e., the wider the wingspan in comparison with the chord), the quicker the kite can accelerate and the more maneuverable it will be.

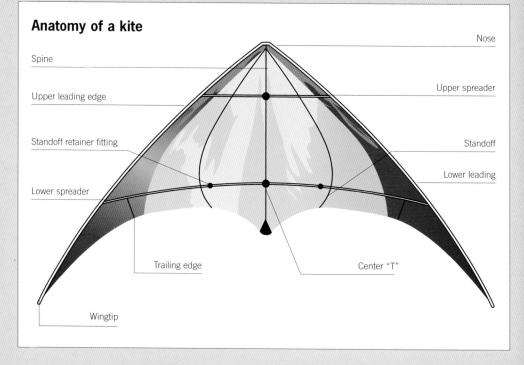

Anatomy of a kite

- Nose
- Spine
- Upper spreader
- Upper leading edge
- Standoff retainer fitting
- Standoff
- Lower leading
- Lower spreader
- Trailing edge
- Center "T"
- Wingtip

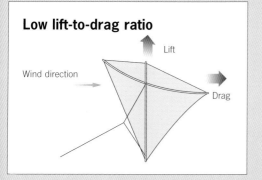

Low lift-to-drag ratio

Lift

Wind direction

Drag

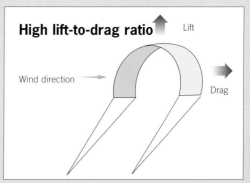

High lift-to-drag ratio

Lift

Wind direction

Drag

Lift-to-drag ratio

Inextricably related to the AR is the lift-to-drag ratio. This is more relevant for power kites but is applicable to all kinds of kites. A kite with a higher AR will have a lower lift-to-drag ratio. Lift is the force on a kite in an upward direction; drag is the force on a kite in a horizontal direction. The lift-to-drag ratio is related to the camber of the kite; a kite with more camber (more curved and C-shaped) has a higher lift-to-drag ratio. What all this means, and what you need to bear in mind when choosing which kite to buy, is that a more curved

kite will create more lift but will be slower in the air, whereas a kite with a narrower profile will not produce so much power for the flier but will fly faster through the air and will also respond more quickly to the flier's actions. A kite's drag is related to the angle of attack (AOA).

AOA

The angle of attack is the angle between the kite's chord and the direction of the wind, and it directly affects the amount of wind the kite can harness. Simply put, a kite with a lower built-in AOA (0–1

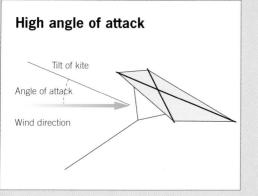

High angle of attack

Tilt of kite

Angle of attack

Wind direction

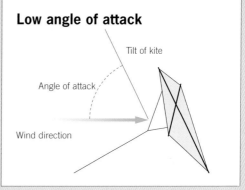

Low angle of attack

Tilt of kite

Angle of attack

Wind direction

degrees) will be almost head-on to the wind when all lines are taut and of equal length. This means that it will be hard to fly delta and single-line kites, and for power kites it will produce less power than for a kite with a higher AOA (4+ degrees).

Materials

In terms of the construction of a basic kite, the only rule is that the materials must be lightweight, so pretty much anything goes – from bamboo and silk to paper and plastic, in any structure that is wind-friendly. A basic kite that you would find in a toy store is probably plastic and no doubt will fly very well. The more technical (power and stunt) kites have benefited from great advance in material design and production over the past three decades.

Sailcloth

The kite sailcloth is usually made from nylon as this is lightweight and durable. Although there are a few different names and hybrids on the market, the nylon commonly used is ripstop, which provides more durability due to extra thread reinforcements, literally stopping the development of any rips. Other materials that can be used to create a kite sailcloth include ripstop polyester (very lightweight), 3-ply polyethylene (very durable) and pre-coated "spinnaker" nylons (in reference to the sailcloths used for the spinnaker sail of a boat). These materials perform perfectly for non-traction kites, but they are not as appropriate for coping with the conditions imposed upon power kites as ripstop nylon.

As ripstop nylon is so suited to the job of forming a windproof kite sail, little other material is needed. However, gauze is used on the leading edge of a land kite; it is needed to let air in to permeate the cells of the kite and inflate it. Dacron is a tough material used to reinforce the side panels of a kite, which improves its longevity. Finally, one-way rubber valves are used on water-relaunchable kites so that blowing up the bladders is easy and the chances of them coming undone and letting out air are slim.

Spars

Spars – also known as batons, spreaders, sticks, rods or longerons – refer to the skeleton-type bars used to fix a kite's shape. Rods must be lightweight yet durable. For high-spec kites, fiberglass or graphite (carbon) is used. Graphite is both lightweight and durable but is quite pricey, especially wrapped graphite (where individual strands of graphite are wrapped together to form the rod). Fiberglass is the slightly cheaper option: solid fiberglass is fairly tough; hollow fiberglass rods are lighter but they can break more easily.

Lines

Most kites have some kind of bridle, and all kites have lines to which they are attached. Dyneema or the very similar Spectra are the polyethylene fibers most commonly used in kite lines. Dyneema is so strong that it is used for bullet-proof clothing. Dyneema and Spectra are expensive and are not as durable as other materials – they can break from friction if you cross lines with other kites. Kevlar is strong but will cut like a knife once the kite is flying and tension is created. Dacron is a better option if flying in team events or near other people, as it is incredibly hard-wearing, although on the negative side Dacron stretches and cannot support as heavy a load as Dyneema and Spectra.

The best option for beginners is blended Spectra/Dyneema and Dacron. If you choose a line that is more delicate and less durable – such as Spectra/Dyneema, which has a low melting point – it will need to be sleeved with Dacron at the ends to increase the knot strength where it is attached to the kite's bridle.

Understanding single-line kites

Kites with only one line are as spectacular-looking in the sky as any other type of kite (often more so), but are often less taxing to fly once the kite is in the air and the wind is behaving. It is perhaps for this reason that single-line kite fliers are often not in the game solely to fly the kites, but actually to make them as well. With so many individual kite makers, it is no surprise that there are loads of variations in kite shapes and materials. Most lightweight materials have found their way into some kind of kite – from bamboo and bark to paper and plastic. Pretty much anything goes when constructing a kite, as long as it is wind-friendly. As a general rule regarding shape, the simpler the kite (for example, delta, diamond or hexagon kites), the easier it is to fly.

Single-line diamond kite

Design

A diamond kite is one of the easiest kites to fly and pretty much the simplest kite you can make – two pieces of paper, a length of bamboo, some tape and some thread all put together will give you a functioning diamond kite.

Size

The overall size of the kite is not important; it is the relationship between the dimensions that matters. For example, if your diamond kite is not symmetrical along its vertical axis it will not fly well; the right-hand side must be of equal length to the left. However, the bigger the kite overall, the less wind is required to fly it and the more stable it will be when it is in the air. Tiny kites are great as decorations but are useless for flying!

Tail

Banners, ribbons, streamers, tassels, drogues, ladders – all are different types of tails made from all sorts of materials. Some kites need tails as an integral part of their design – for example, the hexagon kite – while other kites use tails purely for aesthetics. Tails can be added to a kite to create more drag, resulting in a less twitchy flight and allowing the kite to fly in stronger winds. The diamond kite in the illustration uses a keel, and so eliminates the need for a bridle, meaning that a tail is not strictly necessary. If a diamond does not have a keel, it will need a tail to fly properly.

Control system

Most single-line kites are flown with a simple spool that the line is wound around, making it very easy to lengthen or shorten the lines depending on wind strength. These spools are perfectly suited for kites that are pegged down once airborne. Shaped winders are slightly easier to hold on to if the kite is not going to be pegged down. These are normally plastic with a hollow section, making it easy to hold on to them when the kite is pulling in the air. There is also the option of using a type of winder like that used for extra-long dog leashes – it pulls in your line at the touch of a button.

As for line length, this is a matter of preference, but be aware that flying above 195 ft. (60 m) can be dangerous and is illegal in some countries (check with your local or federal civil aviation authority if your kite is over 5 lb./2.3 kg). Most factory lines are around the 150-ft. (45 m) mark, some are 300 ft. (90 m), and many enthusiasts reach the smoother winds high up with 500-ft. (150 m) lines. Investing in some tangle-resistant kite line is also a good idea and will save you a lot of time if you intend to fly a lot, as factory lines are notoriously difficult to untangle.

Understanding dual-line stunt or sport kites

Stunt kites vary less in design and materials than single-line kites, as they are designed to entertain not with their static form but with the form of their flight. With this single aim in mind, the design of stunt kites has reached its height with the creation of the delta-shape wing with a high bridle and curved leading edges.

Design

Sport kites are delta kites, as they are almost triangular in shape. They are typified by a single spine and have a high aspect ratio (AR), meaning that they are wider than they are long. They generally have a high bridle and curved leading edges. When choosing a sport kite, take into consideration that there will always be a trade-off between stability and maneuverability; what you gain in one you will lose in the other. Essentially, a more precise and stable sport kite has a lower AR, a wider nose, a longer spine below the T (the center of the kite), straight(er) leading edges, a larger billow (sail depth or slackness of sail) and a longer bridle placed nearer the spine and nose of the kite.

The opposite end of these variables will obviously produce a more responsive kite that can perform advanced tricks.

Two more important design features of a sport kite are the shape of the wings and the wingtips. When the wingtips are narrower and pointed at the end and the trailing edges of the kite are significantly cut away, the kite is able to turn more quickly. The wingtips may also be twisted inward, to resist stalling.

Size

For optimum flying, the kite should be as lightweight as possible, but as big as possible so that it will be stable in light wind. Obviously the bigger the kite, the heavier it becomes, especially with the spar weight, so there is a trade-off and an optimum kite size. This relationship can be calculated in an equation of weight divided by area, the result of which is called wing loading. The lower the wing loading, the less wind it will take to launch and fly the kite. The standard 8-ft. (2.5 m) stunt kites generally achieve optimum wing loading.

Control system

There are a variety of methods of holding on to a stunt kite. Simple spools can be used, but the more popular choices are either padded wrist straps or bar-type handles. The strength and length of lines you choose depend upon the size of the kite, the strength of the wind and – if you want to get very serious – whether you want a more responsive kite that will be unforgiving if you make mistakes or one that reacts more slowly but gives you more time to perform your tricks. Line strengths are often given in terms of their breaking strain. A kite with a breaking strain of 200 lb. (90 kg) is on the stronger end of the spectrum and could be used in stronger winds and/or with bigger kites, whereas a line with a breaking strain of between 100 lb. (45 kg) and 150 lb. (70 kg) is about average. Lengths of line for sport kites are between 65–130 ft. (20–40 m), these days usually sitting around the 80-ft. (25 m) mark, with shorter lines used for indoor kiting or congested areas, and longer lines for stacked kites.

Power kites

Power kites have but one aim – to create power for the flier. Just as for stunt kites, the result of this focus is that most power kites loosely fit the same design mold. The design idiosyncrasies that do exist have an appreciable effect on the flying of the kite, so it's useful to understand a bit more about the diversity in power kites in order to choose which kite is right for you.

Power kites have a rectangular-type shape and a broad wingspan with a short chord, and are typified by a strong, rounded leading edge with a pointed trailing edge. It is this airfoil shape that creates lift for the kite in exactly the same way as does the wing of a plane. Simply explained, the shape diverts air downward, meaning that the kite is pushed upward. The curved, convex shape of a traction kite is important for harnessing the wind's power, and, although this is standard across all power kites, how the shape is created differs for land and water kites.

Traction kites can be distinguished by whether they are for use on water or on land. Those used for land-based flying use the wind to become inflated by letting air into the cells of the kite ("ram-air" kites). Kites that are water-relaunchable use a pre-inflated leading edge and inflated batons to create their shape ("leading edge inflatables" or LEIs). Inflatable kites were invented because a ram-air kite crashing on water will let water in through its open gauze area, rendering the kite useless after sitting on water for any length of time (anything over about 10 seconds!).

The second distinction in power kiting is how many lines a kite has. Dual-line kites generally fly faster and are more responsive than quad-line kites, and are also easy for beginners to set up and fly. On the design side, generally two-line kites are not suitable for kite sports as they do not have the two extra "brake" lines and therefore cannot spill any wind if it gets too strong (i.e., they cannot depower easily). However, some enthusiasts still swear by two-line kites, as they are generally quicker to react than four-lines.

Four-line kites offer more control to the flier than two-lines, and are slower in the air. This means they are more stable, which is great for traction sports where you do not want a twitchy kite to which you have to pay loads of attention while you are trying to perfect your maneuvers down at ground level. You are able to hold your kite in a steady position in the power zone with four-lines, which is pretty tricky to achieve with two-line kites. Also, you can adjust the angle of attack by making your brake lines either shorter or longer, to counter the effects of varying wind strength. This becomes more important when you are attached to the kite with a harness. Quad-lined kites make life easier at the time of relaunching, especially on water, as the four lines enable the kite to be flown in reverse.

For traction sports it is generally advisable to use a four-line kite, as you have more control; however, for recreational use two-line kites are perfect – and you can stack these kites for extra power and to create an awe-inspiring sky decoration for spectators! If you can't decide, there are kites that you can change from four to two lines by essentially losing the brake lines. But be warned, using a large kite without its brake lines is not a good idea.

Dual-line ram-air kite (for use on land)

Design

Power kites for use on land are "ram-air" kites. Ram-air kites use the wind to fill their cells and give them form, rather than having a fixed structure like stunt kites. They are constructed with two pieces of material between which there are cells that become inflated in flight by air filtered through the (gauze) leading edge. They do not historically have any batons to assist with holding their form, but some ram-air kites do use a baton, neatly avoiding a complex bridle system. Ram-air power kites are also referred to as soft kites, parafoils or foils.

Foils have a lower AR and a thinner profile than inflatable power kites, meaning that they are generally faster in the air but do not create as much power as a similar-sized inflatable.

The bridle on some ram-air kites can be pretty complex, as it alone is relied upon to create form for the kite. In the case of foils with a leading-edge spar, the lines are attached directly to the kite, which is considerably easier and less daunting for a beginner.

Size

Size does matter. For power kites, size is hugely important as, roughly speaking, the bigger the kite, the more wind power is capable of being harnessed. For sport kites the overall size is less important than the size relationship between the various parts of the kite, as discussed previously, but for power kites both these issues are important.

As two-line kites do not have any brake lines and therefore no depowering capabilities, it is very important to get the size right. The size of power kite you choose is dependent on three variables – your weight, your ability and the wind strength. A kite of 3 ft. (1 m) projected size (the size it is when laid out on the floor) should be fine for a 110-lb. (50 kg) beginner adult flying in average (force 3 or 4) wind, providing the AR is not too low (about 3 would be good). However, as kites differ so much it is crucial to consult the manufacturer's guidelines as to the conditions for which the kite is suitable.

Control system

The same rules apply for the lines of two-line foils as for the lighter sport kites: the bigger the kite, the stronger the wind, the shorter and/or stronger the lines need to be. A pretty standard length for a power kite line is 80 ft. (25 m), but longer lines may also be used in recreational flying if the wind is weak or where objects close by interfere with the wind, allowing the kite to reach the "clean" wind above the objects.

Two-line kites generally fly faster through the air than four-line kites, so it is possible to use longer lines and still fly a fast kite (although four-lines can turn faster). As a general guide to line strength, a 3-ft. (1 m) kite in average winds (force 3 or 4) would be fine flying on around 225-lb. (100 kg) lines and could even work on lines of 170 lb. (75 kg) at lengths of 65–80 ft. (20–25 m).

Just as for stunt kites, padded straps or handles are normally used to fly two-line power kites recreationally. For kite sports, such as buggying or landboarding, it is possible to use a bar for stability and to free up one hand. In this case the bar length needs to fit the kite; a smaller kite needs a smaller bar. You can "tune" the kite by using a different length of bar. If the kite is too twitchy, use a shorter bar, but if it is too slow to react, use a longer bar.

Harnesses can be used with a two-line kite, but make certain you have a quick-release system and that you know how to use it, as a situation can become an emergency in the time it takes for you to shout, "Woohoo, I'm flying!"

Four-line water-relaunchable kite

Design

Inflatable kites are made from one piece of sailcloth, with an inflatable bladder along the entire length of the leading edge. When this is blown up, the kite forms a C-shape, and to hold the structure more rigidly in place a number of inflatable bladders are sewn in across the chord of the kite to act as rigid rods. This airtight and watertight design means that the kite can land on water without becoming waterlogged and, of course, it will not sink. The disadvantage is that, if the kite is flown on land and it comes down hard, the leading edge may split on impact.

Just as for all power kites, inflatables have a high AR (they are much longer than they are wide); for example, an advanced kitesurfer would be comfortable with a kite of around AR 6. An inflatable will usually have a higher AR than a foil; more power is needed to create friction on water than on land. The joy of inflatables is that they do not need bridle lines all over the place, as the inflatable batons hold the kite's shape.

Size

Generally speaking, all traction kites used on water need to be around 40 percent bigger, or one or two sizes bigger – about 6.5 ft. (2 m) – than their land equivalent. Always check the manufacturer's recommendations for the appropriate conditions in which to fly your kite.

As for all power kites, size is related to the ability and weight of the flier, the wind strength and the sport that the kite is being used for. As a conservative guide, a 110-lb. (50 kg) adult in medium wind (force 4) should be comfortable using a 15-ft. (5 m) kite. Be aware that kites behave very differently depending on their design: one kite may generate twice the power of a similar-sized kite because of variants in design.

Inflating a water-relaunchable kite

Control system

The two front lines are often called the main or steering lines, and the two back lines are sometimes called the power or brake lines. The front lines need to be pretty strong, so a breaking strain of around 600 lb. (250 kg) is common at a length of at least 65 ft. (20 m). The back lines are usually the same length as the control lines (unless you adjust them to change the AOA), but they do not need to be quite as strong, as they do not play such a dominant role in harnessing the wind's power.

For water use, a bar is usually used to control the kite. Although bars do not offer quite as much control of the kite as handles, they do offer stability when you are busy attending to your sea- or ground-level activity. They also allow the kite to fly happily on its own at the top of the wind window without any hands on the bar whatsoever – if it is attached to you via a harness! – which is a welcome benefit of the control bar for those tricky situations where you can't deal with everything at once. Make sure you know how to use your harness's quick-release system if you do attach yourself to the kite.

Other equipment

Kite flying is a fantastically basic sport. For all types of kite flying the principles are simple and, for most, so is the equipment needed. You can get away with sparing little thought for specialized equipment when flying many types of single-line or small dual-line kites. Even flying a power kite does not necessitate buying a whole load of extra equipment, but when you get into applied sports such as buggying and surfing, you will need some extra gear, mainly to keep you safe. High speeds – of both the kite and the flier – are involved, so the peripheral equipment becomes as vital as a paddle is to a canoe.

Recreational kiting clothing

You can wear what you like for sports kiting, but in particular it is recommended that you wear some good-quality, 100 percent UV-graded sunglasses, as you spend a lot of time looking up! Thin gloves can be a good idea too if you are playing around with sharp lines. For more strenuous forms of kite flying, it's a good idea to cover your arms and legs in case you get dragged around – wearing knee pads, elbow pads, wrist guards and impact shorts is a smart idea.

Recreational kiting equipment

Although not essential, it is useful to have with you some of the following items: an anemometer (wind speed gauge) for judging wind speed, a stake to peg your kite lines to the ground, a knife in case you need to cut your lines for any reason, and a towel to dry off your equipment before packing it away. It is also a good idea to bring spares of equipment such as spars, lines and even some sailcloth, as well as tape for repairs. If you are very organized you could even bring some flags to delineate the area in which you intend to fly your kite, to warn passersby.

Power kiting clothing

If you are playing around on land, make sure you wear protective clothing (long sleeves, elbow and knee pads, gloves as a minimum), including a helmet. If in water, always wear a flotation jacket and, again, a helmet. Wetsuits are pretty obligatory if you are in the water anywhere in more northern areas; it's freezing, and don't let anyone tell you any different. If you are snow-kiting, wrap yourself up in all the gear you would wear for snowboarding and skiing – waterproof ski/board pants, jacket and gloves, ski socks, goggles/sunglasses, hat and either ski or board boots.

Power kiting equipment

Harnesses attach the kite to your body, allowing your legs to take some of the strain of the power generated by the kite while still allowing your arms to control it. Used with both the bar and handles, harnesses allow your arms to serve you for many more hours than they could previously. Harnesses are a great idea, but beware – they are only for the competent. It is not particularly funny being dragged along attached to a rampant power kite. It happens, even to the experts, but with experience they know how to get out of the situation quickly.

Harnesses attach either around your buttocks, legs and waist (seat harnesses), or simply around your waist (hip or waist harnesses). Waist harnesses are suitable for advanced riders but are not so comfortable for beginners. This is because waist harnesses end up around the armpits if you spend too long with the kite very high in the sky, as a beginner often does. When spending your time riding, as an advanced surfer does, the kite will be much lower to the ground and therefore will not pull the harness up too much. If you decide to change from a seat to a waist harness, bear in mind that your center of gravity will alter and you will have to adjust your riding position to compensate.

All kite harnesses are made from tough nylon and polyester with non-stretch adjustment straps, and all should have stainless steel attachment rings and spreader or reactor bars. Spreader/reactor bars sit across the front of the harness and attach to the kite with either a hook (spreader bar) or a roller (reactor bar). Added useful features are a handle at the back so that the flier can be held down, padding so that the flier is comfortable, and occasionally a knife pocket complete with knife just in case all your other safety features fail (highly unlikely).

The high-end harnesses are worth the extra money. What you lose financially you gain many times over in comfort and longevity. These harnesses are made to fit men, women and children individually, using tough neoprene, protective back supports and essential load-dispersion systems so that the full force of the kite's pull is not focused on one particular part of your body.

2 Understanding the wind

The most crucial piece of equipment you need for kite sports is the wind. Thankfully this costs not a cent and is provided in abundance; however, it is not all plain sailing. You will need to understand the "wind window" in order to get your kite airborne before anything else. The wind is tricky to master and will cause you untold troubles if you try to fight it, or worse, ignore its prerogative to change at will. This chapter will give you an idea of how to gauge wind speed, direction and quality, all of which are important to the kite flier.

The wind window

For a kite to fly it needs to be pushed away from you by the wind while you pull it back. This harnessing of the wind's power can be achieved only if you are upwind of the kite. If you stand downwind of it at any point there is no longer any resistance for the kite to pull against and it will stall (flop around in the sky). This does not, however, apply to five-line kites, which, because of a design feature, can sit slightly upwind and remain in the sky.

The area in which the kite can fly is actually larger than just directly downwind of you. It fans out at nearly 150° horizontally in front of you and 90° from the ground to above your head. At the edges of this window the kite will produce the least amount of power. It follows that, flying in the middle of this window, the kite will generate the most amount of power. The 40 percent in the middle of the window is called the power zone.

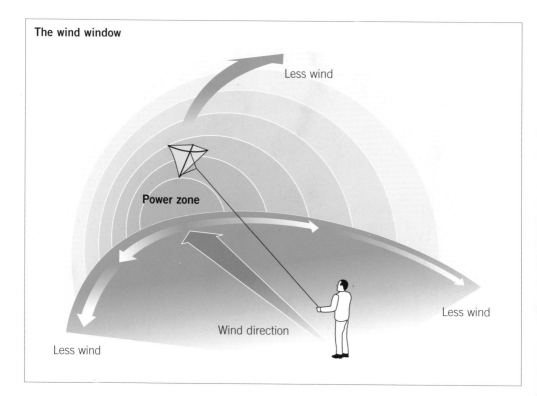

The wind window

Less wind

Power zone

Wind direction

Less wind

Less wind

Wind speed

Weather predictions are readily available in many different media. Turning on your computer/ TV/radio or opening a paper will give you an instant idea of, among other meteorological variations, wind speed. This is a generalized picture of what the wind will be doing, and is useful, as you will not want to venture out if there is no wind predicted or if the wind speed is likely to average more than 30 mph (50 kph). To get a more accurate idea, consult your local media, as local wind effects can cancel or reverse the winds of larger weather patterns.

Once you are at your chosen site, you need to check the wind speed to make sure it is not too strong for your kite, your size, the sport you are practicing, and your ability. Ideally this is done with an anemometer, the more expensive the better. However, do not blindly choose your kite based on your wind meter, as the density of the wind makes a big difference. A summer wind often has less power than a winter one even if it registers the same speed, and "wet" wind will pack more of a punch than a dry one.

You can also gauge wind speed by looking at the signs around you and using Admiral Sir Francis Beaufort's scale. The Beaufort Scale (shown opposite) has been adapted for use on land as well as on water, using a value called "force" for qualifying the speed of the wind. To ensure accuracy when assessing wind speed, try to use the highest indicator possible, for example, the top branches of a tree.

The Beaufort Scale

Description	Wind Speed (Knots)	Wind Speed (KPH)	Force	Land	Water
Calm	0–1	0–1	0	Smoke rises vertically	Water is like a mirror
Light air	2–3	1–5	1	Smoke drifts and indicates direction	Small ripples on water
Light breeze	4–6	6–11	2	Wind felt on face, leaves in trees are moving	Small wavelets
Gentle breeze	7–10	12–19	3	Small flags flap, leaves move constantly	Large wavelets
Moderate breeze	11–16	20–28	4	Small branches move	Some crests at sea
Fresh breeze	17–21	29–38	5	Bushes and small trees sway	Many crests at sea
Strong breeze	22–27	39–49	6	Wind now whistles, most branches in trees moving	Crests everywhere at sea
Near gale	28–33	50–61	7	Whole trees sway, hard to walk into the wind	Much bigger waves
Gale	34–40	62–74	8	Twigs breaking in trees	Foam in well-marked streaks, all boats head in
Strong gale	41–47	75–88	9	Roofs of buildings become damaged	Low visibility due to spray
Storm	48–55	89–102	10	Trees uprooted, buildings become damaged	High seas over 25 ft. (8 m)
Violent storm	56–63	103–117	11	Widespread damage to buildings	High seas over 32 ft. (10 m)
Hurricane	Over 63	Over 117	12	Devastation	High seas over 45 ft. (14 m)

Wind direction

Recognizing the wind direction is, of course, pretty important if you are to keep your kite downwind of you and keep it within the wind window. To find out where the wind is coming from you can look around you at flags, sails or trees, drop some grass, sand or snow and see which way it is blown, or even stick a wet finger in the air and feel which side is coolest. You can tell if the wind is directly behind you if the white noise is equal in both ears. You can also look at clouds for both the current

wind direction and to see the kind of weather that is approaching. Shifts occur all the time, so keep checking exactly where the wind is coming from.

The major concern about wind direction is for kitesurfers on the ocean. It is a dangerous situation if the wind is offshore (that is, blowing from the land to the water), as the kite will always want to drag its flier out to sea. If the kitesurfer is inexperienced he or she may not be able to get back in. Because of diurnal (daily) variation and sea breezes blowing from the cold sea onto the warm land, surfers will usually enjoy at least an afternoon of onshore or cross-onshore wind, depending on which way their shoreline lies and on the strength of local winds. Onshore winds or cross-onshore winds are ideal, as the wind will be less turbulent having traveled over flat sea than if it had traveled over hilly land.

Wind quality

It helps enormously if the wind power you are harnessing is consistent. A lumpy or gusty wind can pull you all over the place or lift you high in the air without any notice, only to dump you down again just as quickly. There is little you can do to control the wind, but there are ways of judging its quality and making sure you choose a day and location where you are most likely to get the wind you are looking for.

Lumpy wind can often be avoided by making sure you have no obstacles upwind of you. An obstacle (such as a tree or building) can create turbulence downwind for seven times its height. An easy way of making sure that an obstacle is far enough away is to hold your thumb out in front of you, with a straight arm. If the offending article seems smaller than your thumbnail, it is far enough away not to affect you.

Gusty wind is created by a variety of weather conditions. Often a weather forecast will predict gusty winds, in which case you are seriously advised not to go flying. Local knowledge is priceless. There may be known areas with gusty conditions and, thankfully, known areas with beautifully clean wind. Although low pressure can occur anywhere and will bring with it its own winds, local winds will often govern particular areas and can override or at least modify these. Local winds, such as sea or land breezes, anabatic or katabatic winds, which blow up hills and down hills respectively, or lake breezes, for example, are mercifully predictable.

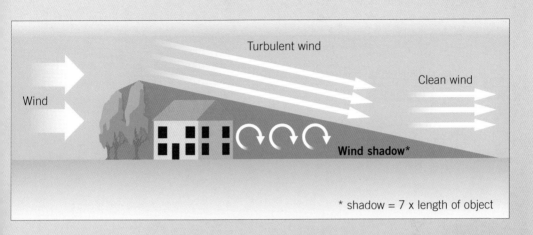

Turbulent wind

Clean wind

Wind

Wind shadow*

* shadow = 7 x length of object

If all else fails, look at the clouds for guidance. A fair day with low cumulus mediocris (piled up, cotton-wool clouds) generally indicate a good, if gusty, breeze, as a cumulus cloud will bring a gust at its leading edge and a lull at its trailing edge. High cirrus uncinus (wispy "mares' tails" clouds) in parallel lines indicate strong winds at altitude and, more likely than not, that an increase in wind speed and change of wind direction are on their way, with or without a front and some nasty weather. Extensive nimbostratus (thick, blanket-like layer clouds) often come with a pleasantly constant wind from a fixed direction, even if they don't create a picture-postcard sunny day for you to play in.

3 Basic flying skills

Kite flying is not hugely taxing, but there is a fair amount to
learn, which takes time. For traction sports such as kitesurfing
or buggying, you do need your flying skills to become second
nature if you are to gain anything more than frustration.
Don't jump straight in with a board in one hand and a
kite in the other. Wait until you can almost land
a kite with your eyes shut.
Learning about the wind first with a single-line kite
is a good idea; then fly a sport kite, as these are
easier to launch and relaunch. Try "sky fly" (hanging
suspended on a huge pole and flying around behind
your kite), if you can find a center that has the
necessary equipment; it's fantastic fun and really helps
you to appreciate the wind window. Even if you are
reasonably proficient at controlling a sport kite, you will still
need to start small with traction kites.

Single-line kite skills

Setup

First you will want to take a look at your kite in the serenity of your home, where there is no wind to flap around your instructions sheet and no long grass or sand in which to lose small parts. There are so many types of single-line kites that it is impossible to offer a guide for setup of each. However, the manufacturer will always give you some instructions. Note the way your kite is packed so that you can disassemble it in the same way. If you made the kite yourself, hopefully it will need little setup on location.

Generally your kite will be packed with its bridle already attached and any rigid spars packed separately. You will need to attach the spars first, then attach the line to the bridle, usually with a lark's-head knot (see page 65), and then the tail if it has one. With some kites you can adjust the bridle to suit the wind conditions: if the wind is strong you can make the bridle lines longer; if it is weak or gusty, make them shorter. A shorter bridle will make the kite easier to launch. If you do adjust the bridle, make sure you mark its original position, as it can take a lot of adjustment to find the appropriate bridle length.

Launch

Running into the wind is not an effective way of launching your kite – more often than not it will dive into the ground. You can either use a friend to help you launch your kite or try alone. If you have the help of a friend, unwind up to 100 ft. (30 m) of line and, standing with your back to the wind, pull gently on the kite line as your friend simply lets go of the kite above his or her head. Pull in the kite if it starts to drop, or let out some line if the wind is strong.

If you are launching alone and the kite is not too large, start by letting it drift out of your hand. Let out some line until the kite drops near the ground. Pull in the line gently to encourage the kite to gain some height, then let out some more line to let the kite drift again. Continue with this process until the kite is flying at the desired height. If the kite is large and you wish to launch it alone, place it on the ground, preferably up against an obstacle so that it can more easily catch the wind when you pull on the line. From this position gently pull on the line when there is a gust of wind. Again, if the kite starts to drift, pull in some line, letting it out as it gains height.

Maneuvers

Single-line kites are not highly maneuverable, but you can control them to an extent by adjusting the line length to keep them in the sky even when facing a changeable wind. If you find your kite is diving around when it is high up, the wind may be too strong, so you will want to reel in the line to find the more gentle winds lower down. If the kite is unstable in the turbulent wind lower down, you

How to launch a single-line kite

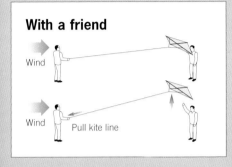

With a friend

Wind

Wind   Pull kite line

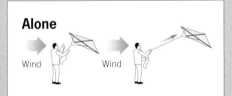

Alone

Wind   Wind

can let out some line to find the cleaner winds higher up. If the kite picks up speed to your left or right, letting out the line will allow it to get back on track. If you want the kite to continue to fly in the direction it is traveling, reeling in the line will accelerate it.

Landing

There are two ways of bringing down your single-line kite. The first is by simply reeling it in. This is fine for smaller kites on days when the wind is not too aggressive. Go slowly, as increasing the tension on your line too quickly will make your kite rise.

The second way is used for bigger kites and involves walking toward it up the line. To bring your kite down this way you need to either ask a friend to hold on to the reel or peg it to the ground. You will then take hold of the line (you will need to wear gloves to protect your hands from the line) and walk along it, gently bringing it down to your height as you go. If you have a friend holding the reel, he or she can gently wind some line around it as you go. When the kite is safely on the ground you can walk back to the reel and wind up your line. You may want to put some weights on the kite to prevent a gust of wind picking it up again.

Stunt-kite skills

Setup

Once you have set up the kite indoors to make sure you know how it all fits together and that you have all the relevant parts, setting up your stunt kite outside should be a breeze. The spars will be packed separately and need to be inserted into their fittings; it is easiest to start with the wing spars and the spine, inserting the spreader spars last to give the kite its shape. You may leave the wing spars and spine attached to the kite when you finish, as you can still fold up the kite in this state as long as you take out the spreaders.

Next you need to unwind your kite lines and attach them to the bridle, using a lark's-head knot (see diagram on page 65). Stand up your kite on its trailing edge so that it is pointing upward and unwind your lines as you walk into the wind.

Dual- and quad-line kites are set up differently from single-line kites as they have preset line lengths rather than a spool that provides varying line lengths. This means that you have to unwind the entire length of line in order to launch the kite, and this makes it more important to choose the right line length for your ability and for the strength of the wind. Note that longer lines (100 ft./30 m) are easier to learn with as they are more forgiving and can be used in lighter winds. Make sure that your lines are of identical length, as controlling your kite will be nearly impossible if they are irregular.

Put the plastic winder in your pocket because, unlike for single-line kites, you do not need it when the kite is flying, only to pack away the lines. If your straps/handles are attached to the lines as they should be, you are ready to fly; if they are not, use the lark's-head knot again. If you need to go back to the kite for any reason, peg your handles to the ground with a ground stake.

Launch

Stunt kites are incredibly aerodynamic, so launching should be as graceful as the kite is light. First check that you are in a suitable location (refer to the safety guidelines in chapter 5). Make sure that the wind is of appropriate strength and directly behind you, and that the kite is directly in front of you. Once the kite is facing upward and the lines are taut, simply pull the lines firmly backward to get the kite airborne. If the wind isn't playing as it should, having a friend hold the kite to start with and gently letting go at your signal should help the launch. Keep your feet shoulder-width apart and your arms low and relaxed, as if you were holding on to the handlebars of a bicycle.

Maneuvers

The joy of adding another line to a kite is that suddenly you are not just standing by, watching an object being blown around helplessly in the sky, but you are able to decide what will happen to the kite and where it will go next. Your relationship with this object high in the sky is now tangibly close and you can decide whether the kite will dive near to the ground and soar up again, whether it will stall and reverse, or whether it will simply glide from left to right. All it takes to exercise

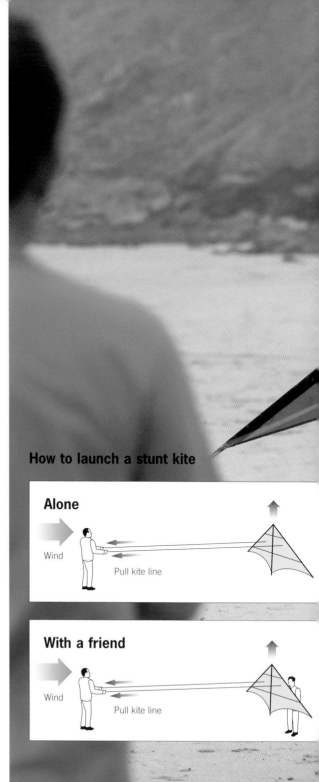

How to launch a stunt kite

Alone

Wind

Pull kite line

With a friend

Wind

Pull kite line

such power is gentle motions of the wrist. To turn the kite left, pull on the left line. To turn the kite right, pull on the right line.

Remember that the kite will lose power at the edge of the wind window and eventually stall, so make sure you always keep the kite within the window. Obviously this means taking care not to fly your kite too far left or right, but also not to fly it too fast upward toward the zenith, as it may propel past your head and essentially upwind of you. Your kite will drop pretty quickly if flown in this way. (See pages 42–43 to better understand the wind window.)

Once you have mastered small left and right movements, try flying your kite in a figure eight, using the entire width of the window, getting a feel for how the kite loses power near the edges of the window. Be aware that the wind direction is changeable, so keep a check on where the edges of the window are.

Try making a faster left turn by pushing your right hand away from you. This stalls the right-hand wingtip by taking the wind out of it and allows the left side to pivot around it. This is a useful skill to master as it eliminates the momentum usually built up by a standard turn, where pulling a line toward you increases the wind pulled into the sail and accelerates the kite through the turn. Once you can control the kite's desire to accelerate, you can work on a whole repertoire of intricate maneuvers that look fantastic in the sky.

▷ **The simple loop** Pull on one line while pushing on the other until the kite makes a complete loop. Don't worry about twisted lines, the kite will fly in just the same way. To untwist, simply pull on the line you have just been pushing and push on the line you have just been pulling – this will make the kite loop back again!

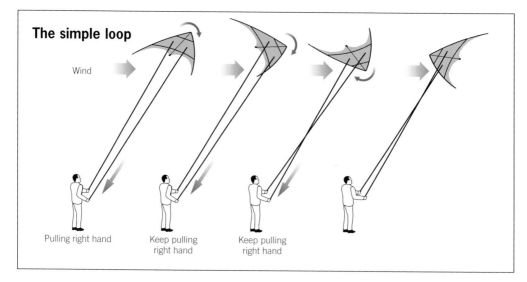

The simple loop

Wind

Pulling right hand   Keep pulling right hand   Keep pulling right hand

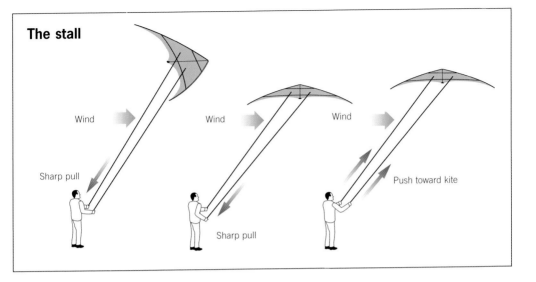

The stall

Wind

Wind

Wind

Sharp pull

Sharp pull

Push toward kite

▷ **The stall** Fly your kite toward the right-hand edge of the window. Pull down quickly and sharply with your left hand. Immediately tug sharply with your right hand, leveling out both tips and pointing the nose of the kite upward. Pushing both hands toward the kite at this point should stall it. To hold the stall, walk toward the kite.

▷ **Wingtip stand** Place the kite on the ground, facing upward, at the edge of the wind window, with the inside wingtip about 1 ft. (30 cm) closer to you than the outside one. Tug gently on the outside line until the outside wingtip begins to lift. You should be able to balance the kite on the inside wingtip.

Landing

Once you have mastered the stall, you have mastered the landing for stunt kites. Simply fly your kite very low at the edge of the wind window and stall it by pushing your hands toward it. It is not essential that the nose of your kite be facing upward when it lands, but it does look tidier. It

looks better still if you throw in a spin stall; having flown your kite low across the window from left to right, slowly turn the kite upward by pulling on the left line. When the nose is facing upward, punch your left hand back to neutral, which will cause the kite to stall and gently sit on the ground. You may have to walk toward the kite to hold the stall long enough for the kite to settle on the ground.

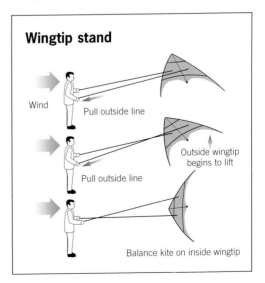

Wingtip stand

Wind

Pull outside line

Pull outside line

Outside wingtip begins to lift

Balance kite on inside wingtip

Power kite skills

Setup

Having gone through the manufacturer's instructions at home and checked that your kite is in good working condition, that all the parts are there, and that they all fit together as they should, you are now ready to take to the great outdoors.

Get your kite out

▷ Point your kite downwind so that it can flap away as you are getting it ready or inflating it. If you battle with the wind you will always lose, so work with it, rather than against it!

▷ Pin down your kite to prevent it blowing away – fold over 6–8 in. (15–20 cm) of the upwind tip and place sand/dirt/snow on the exposed backside of the kite.

▷ If you have a land kite, lay it out on its back with the trailing edge closest to the flier, weighting the upwind wingtip.

▷ If you have an inflatable kite, blow up the bladders first, then the leading edge. When you have finished, place the kite upside down with its back to the wind, pinning it down again just inside the leading edge.

Lay out your lines upwind of your kite

▷ Place the ends of the lines next to the appropriate attachment points on your kite.

▷ Walk all the way up the lines, gently separating them.

▷ If you have a four-line kite, place the power lines either both on the outside or both on the inside of the main lines. Whichever you choose, do the same every time you set up your kite to avoid mistakes.

Attach your lines to the kite

▷ If your lines are not attached to the kite, you will need to attach them. You may decide to leave your lines attached when you pack up, which often makes unwinding the lines easier.

▷ Most kite lines are attached using a lark's-head knot and are color coded to ensure each line attaches to the right place on the kite.

▷ Remember that your inflatable kite is upside down, so you need to attach your bar (if you are using one) upside down too!

▷ Walk back down your lines to check that they are not tangled, have no snags in them, and are of equal length.

Tips for setting up

▷ Use just enough sand/dirt/other material to weigh your kite down; using excess only puts unnecessary strain on the kite. The material on the inside of the kite will wear more quickly, so do not place anything on the inside.

▷ You can tune a four-line kite to accommodate slightly stronger winds by attaching the leading-edge lines closer to the kite and the trailing-edge lines farther away from the kite for less power, and vice versa for lighter winds.

▷ It is easier to lay your lines out in the same direction as the wind so they do not get blown out of place if the wind is strong. However, in lighter winds you can get away with laying them out in the position from which you intend to launch them.

Tying a lark's-head knot

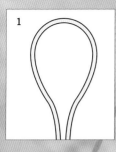

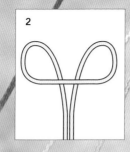

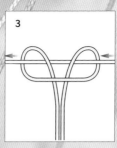

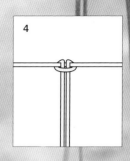

Create a loop by folding over a section of line (most kite lines already have a loop at the end).

Push the loop down so it collapses backwards.

Now thread a second line through the two loops.

Pull down on the original line to tighten the knot.

Launch

This is the point at which you really should have a friend present if you are flying a LEI; launching with someone to help you is incomparably easier than launching alone. There are a variety of different ways to launch your kite that are worth playing around with in weak winds. However, the methods below are the most safety-conscious when the main aim is to minimize the impact of a strong and unpredictable wind on a low-flying kite.

Getting into position

▷ Check the safety guidelines in chapter 5. Make sure you are clear of any obstacles and that there is sufficient space downwind in case you get dragged.

▷ For normal wind conditions, you will launch from the edge of the wind window. This means walking with your kite controls until you reach a position where the wind is not directly behind you but coming from your left or right and slightly behind you.

Assisted launching of an inflatable kite

1 Your helpful partner should hold the kite in front of him or her by its leading edge. Your partner should keep the leading edge pointing to the outside of the wind window.

2 Move backward until there is tension in the flying lines. They should keep still as you move into position.

3 When you give the command your partner should gently let go of the kite. He or she shouldn't throw the kite in the air, just release it at head height.

4 Steer the kite gradually upward to the zenith. Keep the kite at the outside of the window.

3

Tips for launching your kite

▷ Prearrange some simple hand signals with your helper to communicate *I'm ready*, *Let go*, *Abort!*, as it is often too hard to hear in the wind.

▷ Make sure your helper keeps an eye on the kite and moves as quickly as possible to a safe position – either much farther downwind of your kite or, preferably, upwind behind you.

▷ Do not be tempted to lift your arms to accelerate the launch, but if the wind is weak, you may have to step back a bit as the kite starts to lift.

▷ Keep your feet apart, knees bent and arms low for balance and control.

▷ Be ready to brace against the pull of the kite.

▷ Try not to get sand, etc., on the inside tip of your kite when solo launching, as this makes the kite harder to launch and control.

Solo launching of an inflatable kite

1 Only solo launch an inflatable if you absolutely have to. Assisted launching is easier and considerably safer.

2 Put the kite on its side. Face it always to the outside of the wind window so that the leading edge faces into the wind.

3 Fold over the lower tip and weight it with sand or dirt. Make sure that there is sufficient weight to keep the kite in place until you are ready to launch it.

4 Move into position to create tension in the line. Be prepared to brace yourself for the pull of the kite as you begin to create tension.

5 As the weight slides off, fly the kite gradually up to the safety of the zenith. The weight should slide off as you create tension and the kite begins to lift. Steer the kite gradually upward, keeping it at the edge of the wind window if the wind is average to strong, until it reaches the zenith.

Launching a ram-air kite

You do not need assistance when launching a foil. In fact, having someone hold your kite for you can often be a hindrance.

1 Place the kite in position depending on the wind strength. If the wind is strong, you need to place

your kite on its back with its leading edge facing toward the outside of the wind window (so the kite lies lengthways in line with the direction of the wind). Fold over a small section of the upwind tip and pin it down with sand/dirt. (Folding over the edge before piling sand on it means that the abrasive grit does not damage the more delicate underside of the kite.) If the wind is weak, place it on its back with the leading edge facing downwind and weight it on both tips.

   NB If you are using a stake or someone is holding on to the brake lines, the kite does not need to be pinned down.

2 Walk backward to take up the slack of the lines.

3 Pull gently on both lines attached to the leading edge if your kite is in position for weak wind, or on the downwind tip if your kite is weighted on the upwind tip, ready to fly to the outside of the wind window.

4 Step back slightly until the kite is fully inflated and sitting upright, then pull equally with both hands to lift the kite.

5 Steer the kite gradually upward to the zenith at the edge of the wind window if the wind is strong.

   NB If your kite has a spar, you may need to place it so that you can easily pull it around to face its leading edge into the wind. This may mean placing it on its back in stronger wind so that you can flip it over when you are ready, or simply at an angle to the wind on its front so that you can pull it to face more into the wind when you are ready.

How to launch a ram-air kite

Wind Window

Wind

Kite leading edge

Wind Window

Pull on leading-edge lines

Wind

Wind Window

Step back slightly until the kite is fully inflated and sitting upright, then pull equally with both hands to lift the kite

Wind

Relaunching

Relaunching your foil on land is pretty straightforward, as you can walk the lines into position so that you can go through the launching procedure again, as outlined above. Relaunching your foil in water is not easy, however, and your chances of success are vastly reduced by the length of time it takes you to try, as your kite will quickly become waterlogged. The best advice is not to bother using a ram-air on water at all. Whichever kite you are relaunching, whether on land or water, make sure you never switch around your handles or the bar to try to untwist a line that has become twisted from kite loops. The kite will perform in just the same way whether or not it is upside down or has twists in the line from spinning (you can untwist it by flying more loops).

Relaunching a ram-air

If your kite has landed facing upward, relaunch just as if you were launching for the first time, taking care to avoid flying your kite directly downwind if the wind is strong, as you are likely to get dragged off your feet.

If your kite has landed upside down, you can reverse-launch your kite if you are using handles (using a bar is possible but not recommended).

If you crash your LEI while out on the water, you will have to relaunch on water. This is straightforward if your kite lands on its trailing edge; simply make sure the lines aren't tangled and that the kite is not right in the center of the wind window (swim sideways if it is), and pull back on the control bar to lift the kite. If your kite lands on its side, front or back, it takes more effort to relaunch.

Relaunching an inflatable on water

▷ Make sure the lines aren't tangled or around you or your board.
▷ Position the kite on its side, facing toward the edge of the wind window.
▷ If the kite has landed on its leading edge with its belly facing you, you need to swim at it hard so that it folds over onto its back. From this position you can pull on one side of the bar so that the kite flips up onto its side.
▷ If the kite has landed leading edge down, facing you, you need to turn it around so that the belly is facing you. This is not easy and you may have to haul the kite in toward you to sort it out. Once you have achieved this, you can fold it onto its back by swimming at it, as above, and then pull on one side of the bar to put it on its side.
▷ If the kite has landed on its side facing into the center of the wind window, swim into a position that faces the kite to the outside of the window. You can also slowly steer the kite into position even when it is in the water.
▷ Pull the line attached to the upper wingtip to slowly lift the kite.
▷ Pulling on the upper line too hard will send the kite straight into the power zone and you straight into the air, so go tentatively.

Reverse launching

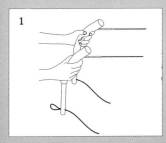

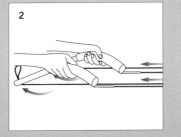

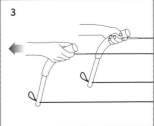

Hold the handles the right way up, even though the kite is upside down.

To reverse the kite, point your thumbs at the kite, rotating your wrists so that you pull the brake lines towards you.

As the kite rises, pull on one side so that the kite spins and faces upwards.

Maneuvers

First, make sure you position your body well. You want to keep everything low so that you are ready to absorb any pull from the kite rather than letting it drag you off your feet. Place your feet shoulder-width apart, flex your knees and keep your weight on your heels. Keep your arms low, in the position you would use to hold handlebars on a bike. While you are learning, keep your eyes trained on your kite.

Your first aim is to keep the kite hovering directly above you, at the zenith. This is achieved by using the smallest of steering movements to correct any attempt the kite makes to fly to one side or the other. Think of playing the piano rather than the drums.

Steering is achieved in the same way for all dual- and quad-line kites: to turn the kite left, pull down and toward you on the left line; to turn the kite right pull the right line. If you have a four-line kite with handles, pull on the left handle to go left; if you have a bar, pull on the left side. When flying more powerful kites you will naturally push with the opposite hand to balance your body, which further assists in turning the kite. This is also a useful technique for more advanced fliers who wish to make a quicker turn. The pushing motion stalls one side of the kite and allows the other side to pivot around it, executing a faster turn. Make sure you use a push/pull motion, as using an up/down motion will achieve nothing! Keep your movements smooth and slow. Large kites will often have a delay in their response to your actions, meaning that you will end up oversteering and losing control if your movements are hurried or jerky. Finally, keep your shoulders parallel rather than using your whole body to steer.

Remember to keep the kite within the wind window. Although five-line kites extend the size of your wind window by allowing you to fly your kite slightly past your head (essentially upwind), most kites will drop if they are pushed that little bit too far.

Once you can turn left and right, try some figure eights across the top of the window, near the zenith. As you gain confidence, try flying the kite closer to the power zone while shaping figure eights. Feel the points at which the kite's pull is the strongest, when it is closest to the center of the wind window. It is these figure eights that you will use to build up power in traction-kite sports, timing your movements to coincide with your kite's flying through the strongest and weakest points of the window.

Flying a four-line kite with handles

You have the greatest control of your kite when using four lines and handles. The main lines are attached to the top of the handles, where your thumbs are. The rear lines are attached to the bottom of the handles. To make a sharper turn you can use the rear lines to help stall one side of the kite and pivot the rest of the kite around it. For example, to turn sharply left, pull on the left handle with extra pull to the rear line. This is achieved by pointing the top of the handle (where your thumb is) toward the kite. In strong winds it is pretty tricky trying to point your thumbs toward a powerful kite and twist the lower half of your hand toward you while hanging on for all you're worth, but it does become more natural with practice.

Tip

Be aware that it takes an unsymmetrical movement to turn left and right when flying at the edge of the wind window.

Flying a four-line kite with a bar

Using a bar can make life easier, as the kite is more stable (depending on whether the kite is a fixed-power or depowerable kite) and you can hold on with only one hand when you need to, and you can hook into a harness with a safety system. The flip side of this is that you will often have less control of your kite, so your movements take longer to correct, resulting in a magnification of the effects of slightly awkward steering.

Using a bar to steer is as straightforward as using two handles; pulling toward you with your left hand while pushing with your right will turn the kite left, and vice versa. If you are flying a depowerable kite (where the kite's angle of attack can be changed while in flight), once you are hooked into your harness with a safety system, you can pull the whole bar toward you to increase the power of the kite (the harness will hold steady the rear lines). Pushing the bar away from you will effectively apply the rear lines, which spill some of the wind's power.

Landing

There are a variety of ways of landing small, maneuverable kites using stalls, which are completely impractical for larger inflatable kites. Although brake lines assist in the landing of four-line kites, both two- and four-line power kites are pretty tricky to land competently, even more so when using a bar rather than handles.

Landing an inflatable is more difficult than landing a ram-air kite for the simple reason that the fixed-form inflatable is always itching to jump up and fly away. The ram-air kite without the wind

in its cells will sit deflated and lifeless once you put it in a safe position. This means that it's a good idea to find someone to help you land your inflatable even if you managed the launch solo. Luckily, kite fliers are a generous subsection of society and will all help one another to land kites whether they know each other or not.

Assisted landing of your power kite

▷ If your helper is a nonflier, remember to brief him or her to stay back behind the kite until it is within catching distance.

▷ Bring the kite to the edge of the wind window. It is possible to land it in the middle of the window if winds are very light.

▷ Gently steer it down for your helpful buddy to catch it. Once he has hold of the kite, take a few steps forward to release the tension on the lines. He should hold the kite lightly by its leading edge and let it flap downwind of him.

▷ Leave your control system on the ground as you quickly go to secure your kite. Just as you secured it before launching, weight your kite with non-sharp objects (place your inflatable kite upside down, leading edge facing upwind).

Solo landing of a ram-air kite

▷ There are a few different ways to solo land a kite, the most popular being reverse landing for four-line kites – simply apply the brake lines to reverse the kite until it comes to rest on the ground (impossible for kites with only two lines). The following guide offers the most straightforward method for all types of kite.

▷ Fly the kite in a low horizontal pass. If the wind

is strong, use only the edge of the wind window.

▷ The kite will lose power at the edge of the window and will come to rest. The kite will probably land on its back.

▷ Loosen any tension in the lines by taking a step forward. Make sure you give extra slack to whichever edge is farther away from you.

▷ Retrieve your kite as quickly as possible. If you have a stake, use it to stop the kite blowing away; pin down any other equipment you may have, such as harness loops, rear (brake) lines or one line of a two-line kite.

Solo landing of an inflatable kite

It is extremely difficult and risky to solo land an inflatable kite and you are strongly advised not to attempt it. If your kite has a solo-landing device, follow the manufacturer's guidelines, making sure you are fully practiced in light winds before attempting the landing in higher winds. Remember to unhook from your harness before landing your kite!

Packing up

When you pack up your kite, treat it with love. Folded material becomes weaker over time, so roll the kite up rather than folding it. If your kite has sand or dirt on it, brush off as much as you can on site as both are abrasive. If your kite is still wet, hang it out to dry when you get home to avoid mildew and odors, brushing off any dried sand or dirt before packing it up again. Kite lines should be wound up with care as even little knots cause considerable weakness to the line. Washing your line in fresh water if you have been flying in the ocean will prevent salt erosion. If you decide to wash your kite, use a soft cloth and make sure it is dry before packing it away.

4 Kite sports

The simple rule of adding wind to many activities involving fast movement has resulted in several fantastic kite sports. The development of the technical knowledge as well as appropriate materials to create traction kites has paved the way for these sports. The best-known kite sports are kitesurfing (riding on a surfboard in water being pulled by a kite) kite buggying (riding on land in a three-wheeled buggy pulled by a kite) and kite landboarding (riding on a skateboard on land being pulled by a kite). Others include scudding, where the flyer is dragged on his or her feet, and body dragging where he or she is dragged in the water. Kite skating, snow-kiting, kite skiing and kite kayaking are some of the lesser-known high-adrenaline games to play! This chapter discusses just a few of the most popular sports and offers guidelines on how to get started.

General skills

Your basic itinerary will be as follows:

▷ Learn how to set up, launch, control and land your kite (chapter 3). (Learning how to fly a sport kite first is a good idea.)

▷ Learn to scud. Allow the kite to pull you forward so that you skid (hopefully in a controlled manner) on your feet. Keep your feet apart and your arms low.

▷ Learn to use the type of kite and control system suited to your sport of choice, in the right environment. You will use either a bar and harness or handles (with or without a harness). The two systems are very different and need to be mastered independently. You will need to fly your kite in the water if you are going to kitesurf (body dragging).

▷ Learn to kitesurf, snow-kite, kite buggy and landboard!

Thankfully the learning curve for kiting and kite sports is relatively steep in comparison with many other sports; most beginners will be able to control a two- or four-line delta kite within a couple of hours. Becoming a vaguely proficient sport kite flier takes anything from three hours to a month of constant flying, but learning every maneuver is a lifetime's endeavor.

The addition of power to the equation means that learning to control a traction kite takes slightly longer than learning to control a sport kite. An instructor is not just an added bonus in speeding along your learning process with power

kites, but a necessity, as your simple mistakes could cause serious injury. As a rough guide, it will take the average beginner around three hours of flying with an instructor before being anywhere near ready to try any traction sports.

Although traction-kite sports skills vary considerably, there are constants. First, you will need to either tack or jibe once you start moving. Just as in sailing, tacking and jibing are turning back and forth across the wind. Tacking is when the vessel points downwind through the turn (when the tail of the vessel passes through the eye of the wind), and jibing is when it turns upwind (when the nose of the vessel passes through the eye of the wind). You will need to tack or jibe so that you can travel back and forth across the wind and end up in the same place that you started. Ideally, you want to travel at 90° to the direction of the wind so that you don't travel too far downwind and have to spend a lot of effort getting upwind again. Trying to get upwind can be a bit of a labor of love; keep the kite high and keep your "vessel" pointed as far upwind as possible. Bear in mind that you cannot travel directly upwind or downwind. Although it is possible to travel directly downwind, you will quickly gain a lot of speed until you almost catch up with your kite, meaning that it loses tension and stops generating power.

Second, to move in a regular direction you want to try to "lock" your kite in position, usually at about a 45° angle from the ground. This gives a smooth and constant pull, which makes life a lot easier for you. If the wind is stronger you may need to fly the kite higher, or if it is weaker, a little lower.

However, neither a very high kite nor a very low kite is ideal, for they will create too much lateral/vertical pull respectively.

Finally, with all kite sports, when you are moving, you must fly your kite on only one side of the wind window until you turn and change direction. If you imagine that directly above you is 12 o'clock, you cannot fly your kite across the window from, say, 10 to 2 o'clock while traveling in one direction otherwise the kite will fly behind you and you will lose power and control. The kite must always stay the same side of 12 o'clock to keep you traveling in the same direction. Only when you decide to tack or jibe will you take the kite from, say, 10 o'clock up to 12 o'clock and on to, say, 2 o'clock.

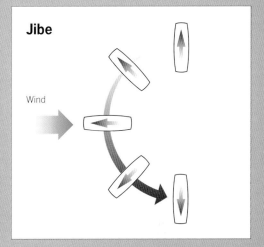

Jibe

Wind

Jibing is when the vessel turns upwind (when the nose of the vessel passes through the eye of the wind).

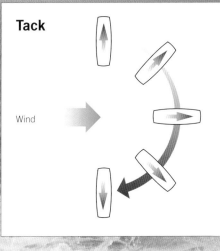

Tack

Wind

Tacking is when the vessel points downwind through the turn (when the tail of the vessel passes through the eye of the wind).

General equipment

You will need different setups for different sports and wind conditions. Never try to make do with an oversized kite on a windy day, or a land-based kite for water-based flying. Check the safety section on pages 118–123 for the appropriate equipment you should consider for each sport.

The setup guidelines offered in this chapter are based on 80-ft. (25 m) long lines, and kite sizes are actual rather than projected. The guides are based on the flying capabilities of a four-line kite with a depowering system. These kites can cope with 5 mph (8 kph) stronger winds than their less sophisticated two-line relatives, which do not have depowering capabilities.

NB Remember that the higher the AR (aspect ratio; see page 14), the less stable but more responsive the kite will be. The guidelines that follow indicate only the overall size of the kite, not its dimensions. Therefore, for beginners and children, make sure that the chord is not too thin in relation to the wingspan; otherwise the kite will be harder to control. A good beginner's kite aspect ratio would be 3, for example, a 6-ft. (180 cm) wingspan to a 2-ft. (60 cm) chord depth (resulting in a 3-ft./1 m kite).

Scudding

Land-based traction sports

Recreational kiting

Although power kites have been designed with specific sports in mind, there is no reason why you can't just take your kite up a hill and fly it with no board, skates or buggy. Scudding (skidding) is generally what happens when you take your kite out in any sort of wind; the kite drags you forward when you fly it through the power zone. It is easy to get airborne with a power kite if it is the right size, so jumping is an obvious progression from scudding.

Equipment

Check with the manufacturer or retailer for the size of kite you should be using for your weight and ability and the strength of the wind. As a rough guide, a beginner of around 145 lb. (65 kg) should be comfortable with a 5-ft. (1.5 m) square kite in force 3 winds (average wind strength). As the kite does not have to power anything but you, it does not need to be as big as for other sports. However, if you intend getting any air, you will be using the kite's lift rather than its lateral pull to get airborne, meaning that you will use the kite only at the top of the wind window. This means you need a bigger kite than if you were using the maximum power generated from the whole of the window. For recreational flying, it doesn't matter if you use a two- or four-line kite.

As for lines and handles/bars, pretty much anything goes! If you are using your kite recreationally to practice for other sports, it is useful to use the same setup. For example, use a bar and harness if you are practicing for kitesurfing, or handles if you are practicing for buggying. Otherwise, it really doesn't matter what you choose to help you hold on to your kite, as long as you (a) do hold on to it, and (b) do not attach it to yourself without an emergency release system. Make sure you are wearing protective gear and have checked that the area is safe to fly in (see page 120).

Basic skills

Once you have mastered figure eights and are used to how quickly your kite turns and how much power is generated, try practicing harnessing your kite's power to pick you up off the ground. This is an indispensable skill for power-kite sports, as they all need an initial controlled burst of power to get you and your chosen method of transportation moving. From a sitting position, with your feet on the ground in front of you and your knees bent, dip the kite hard down to either the left or right, immediately bringing it back up almost to the zenith. Practice this until the power generated by dipping the kite pulls you easily onto your feet.

"Getting air" is a possible next progression, where you use the kite's power to lift you off the ground. Jumping with a kite can lift you to a considerable height – and drop you pretty quickly. For this reason, don't try it until you are with an instructor and on soft land. The basic idea is to position the kite low down and on the right side of the wind window. You need to run to the right at the same time as you fly the kite swiftly left, back up to the zenith. Using a slope to jump off will give you extra lift; fly the kite away from the slope as you run in the same direction. Swing the kite back toward the slope as you run away from it and off the edge of the slope. It takes a while to get the timing right for this, but once you have it, you can fly the kite back away from the slope again to prolong your jump.

Kite buggying/parakarting

Buggying is a fitting progression from land-based recreational flying, as it is not too tricky for the average simple adrenaline-crazed enthusiast. Buggying can take place anywhere with flat open spaces and involves a power kite, usually a harness, and a single-seater buggy. The standard kite buggy, developed from Peter Lynn's design, is three-wheeled, with a very low center of gravity.

You steer the buggy with your feet, leaving your hands free to fly the kite.

Equipment

Once accessible only to the truly committed because of their prohibitive cost, buggies are now available for amateurs to use. Design has improved by leaps and bounds, meaning that you have more choices to make when buying equipment. Will you be using your buggy on a pebble beach or on sand? Will you be racing your buggy or using it for freestyle? Luckily you can customize most buggies so you don't have to commit yourself totally when you buy one, changing, for example, the wheels for larger ones to cope with sand, or the length of the buggy to cope with longer or shorter legs. Start with a basic small buggy with wheels big enough for the terrain you intend to use it on, making sure that the ground clearance of the seat is high enough if you are using it on rough terrain. Bigger buggies allow you to go faster with bigger kites, but you can always use your smaller buggy for freestyle once you progress, so it will never be outgrown!

Once you have customized your buggy, you will need a land-based kite, preferably with four lines. It is true that kites with two lines are easier to learn on, but four-lines have the necessary safety features for traction sports and can lock the kite into position, meaning you can focus more on the buggy rather than the kite. As a rough guide, a 145-lb. (65 kg) beginner should suit a 13-ft. (4 m) square kite in force 3 winds (average wind speed). If you cannot comfortably hold on to a kite when standing, it is too big.

You will need appropriate safety gear: helmet, pads, sunglasses, gloves, sturdy shoes, long-sleeved clothing and, once you get the hang of it, a harness to give your arms a rest. You can use a harness with handles as well as a bar, as handles attach to a strap line that hooks under the harness bar. If you do choose to use a harness, make sure it's not bulky, as this is uncomfortable when sitting in a buggy seat.

Basic skills

Kite buggying can be a more natural progression from recreational flying than straight to surfing or boarding if you have not already had some type of boarding experience. At least everyone is pretty good at sitting down, which is all you have to do to start with.

How to set yourself up The wind direction will determine the direction in which you will travel, as you want to travel back and forth across the wind. So, to start, point the nose of your buggy at about a 30° angle from directly downwind. If the wind is stronger you can increase this angle up to 70°. Place the buggy upwind of yourself so you don't fall on top of it when launching. Launch the kite and sit it either in the zenith or at the edge of the wind window if lofting is a particular threat. While the kite hovers, sit down in the buggy, keeping one foot on the ground to stop it rolling.

How to set yourself up

How to get moving Always considering the strength of the wind, you need to bring the kite down slowly into the power zone only so far as to start to make you move. If you are facing 30° to the right of the wind direction, fly your kite only on the right-hand side of the window. If you fly it to the left the kite will end up behind you and either rip you out of your buggy or run over your arm backward. Once you are ready, put both feet on the foot pegs, which will allow your buggy to move and will give you the ability to steer.

Once you are moving, steer your buggy slightly further across the direction of the wind at an angle of around 80°– 90° so that you do not end up going downwind too far. Try to fly the kite in a stable position in the wind window – wherever it creates sufficient pull to move your buggy (45° to the ground is a good position). If the wind is very weak you may have to fly the kite in a sine wave to build up power, but make sure you fly it on the side of the wind window that you are facing, rather than crossing the whole window, which will result in the kite flying behind you.

How to stop Slowing down and stopping involve two actions – first, fly the kite higher in the wind window; second, steer the buggy upwind. If this is done gradually, the stop will be smooth. If you are too aggressive, however, the stop will be quick and will involve your flying out of the buggy backward. As you progress, you can synchronize flying your kite upward with a faster turn upwind of your buggy, creating a skidded stop as in skiing or hockey.

Maneuvers

How to turn It may help you to choose two reference points 90° to the wind direction at which you can aim when turning, as the apparent wind when you are moving in your buggy can confuse you and you may lose the feel for the wind direction. Turning across the wind is a pretty simple exercise compared to everything else you have achieved by this point. Your aim is to both turn your buggy around and start flying your kite on the other side of your body.

First, slow down by flying the kite higher in the window. Do not stop, but when traveling slowly and in control, steer the buggy downwind quite aggressively so as not to come to a complete standstill until you are facing your opposite reference point. Dip your kite into the power zone on the other side of your body to build up some speed again, and then either lock your kite into position as before or fly a few sine waves until you

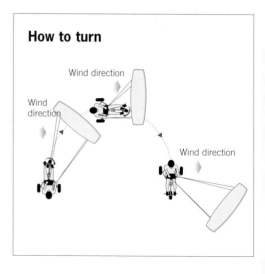

How to turn

Wind direction

Wind direction

Wind direction

build up speed. Essentially you are turning the kite just before the buggy, and turning the buggy as tightly as you can.

How to get upwind You may not have the best time trying to get upwind in a buggy. One problem is that you still have to turn downwind to change direction (until your skills are honed enough for an upwind turn), often resulting in your losing any ground you have just managed to claw back from riding slightly upwind before the turn. This means you will frequently take two steps forward and one step back. On the more positive side, it does get easier the more you do it. You will need to keep your kite higher in the window than the standard 45° and your buggy pointing as far upwind as you can manage without losing momentum or being dragged/pulled over sideways. Do not fly your kite too high as it may wander behind you and pull you out of your buggy. A slightly lower kite will also maintain the power you need to keep upwind.

How to ride on two wheels To add a bit of style and get a feel for how the buggy moves, try riding on two wheels. This is achieved by turning the buggy slightly upwind while traveling at speed. As the buggy is pulled sideways, turn the wheel sharply away from the kite while leaning toward the kite. The buggy should lift onto two wheels and you should be able to maintain this position with practice and good kite control.

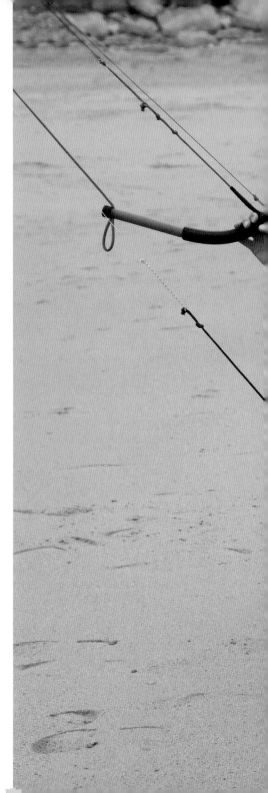

Kite landboarding

Kite landboarding is not too tricky a progression from
recreational flying if you have some experience of riding a
board, whether it be a skate-, surf- or snowboard. It is handy
that you can jump off at any point and regain control should
you feel wobbly.

Equipment

Most landboards these days are twin-directional, meaning that
they are built symmetrically for riding both ways. This means
that you will not have to set up your foot straps for a right- or
left-footed riding preference, if you have one (although they may
have a bias, with one foot strap set up with a more forward
angle than the other). When choosing a landboard you need to
decide whether you intend to ride on a smooth or rugged
surface, and whether you are aiming to perfect airborne tricks
or to remain stuck on the ground.

If air time is what you are looking for, choose a light and
concave board (a board with camber) that will flex to soften
your landings. Choose relatively loose trucks so that your wheels
are not fastened to your board too rigidly, and set your stance

just within your shoulder width. If you are looking to ride fast, choose a longer deck and use a wider stance, combining this with stiff trucks so that you do not wobble at speed.

As for the wheels, choose bigger tires with extra grip for rugged ground and sand. Don't forget your safety equipment and a harness once you are confident (either a seat harness, which is easier for intermediates, or a waist harness for the advanced).

The kite you choose should be designed for land use and, as for buggying, you should be able to fly it comfortably while standing still. As a very rough guide, a 145-lb. (65 kg) beginner could use a 15-ft. (4.5 m) kite in force 3 winds.

Basic skills

Have a practice on the landboard on a slight hill before you fly with it, to get a feel for how it responds to your weight shifting and pressuring your toes and heels. If you do not know whether you are goofy (right foot forward) or regular (left foot forward), work out from this practice which foot feels more comfortable leading. If you really don't know, get someone to push you from behind when you are not expecting it, and whichever foot you fall onto first is generally the best foot for you to put forward. If you still don't know, don't worry, as you will probably eventually end up riding with both feet leading.

How to set yourself up As for all kite sports, the wind direction will determine the direction in which you will travel. You want to travel back and forth across the wind, with your back upwind and your front facing downwind, where the kite will be. To start, place your board at about a 60° angle from

downwind, with the toe side more downwind and the heel side upwind. Launch the kite and sit it either in the zenith or at the edge of the wind window if lofting is a particular threat. While the kite hovers, place your feet in the straps. Sort out your basic stance – flex your knees, put your weight slightly over your back foot and keep your arms low. Try not to bend at the waist so that your backside is sticking out, as you can't balance so well in that position. You are now ready to go.

How to get moving Always considering the strength of the wind, bring the kite down slowly into the power zone, to the right-hand side if you are goofy, or left if regular. Once the board starts moving, lean back to brace against the pull of the kite. You may have to fly a few sine waves to generate power, but then you should be able to lock the kite into position at 45° from the ground. You now need to steer the board so that you ride across the wind rather than too far downwind (to save a big walk back upwind to get back to where you started). To turn the board away from the kite, pressure your heels and lean back.

How to stop Stopping is achieved in much the same way as for buggying: steer the kite upward toward the zenith while steering the board upwind. As in buggying, do not be too aggressive to start with, as you will be thrown off your board. As you progress, the kite's upward flight and the board's upwind turn can be timed to produce a skidded stop (flex even more at your knees and really push down your heels to produce the skid). Note that on rugged terrain you are unlikely to produce a skid however hard you dig your heels in.

How to stop

Wind direction

Wind direction

Wind direction

Maneuvers

How to turn The good news is you don't have to turn the board if you are riding a twin-directional board. To ride in the opposite direction all you have to do is lift the kite to the zenith until your board comes to a stop, then lower the kite into the other side of the power zone. The board will then start moving in the opposite direction. Again, fly some sine waves (keeping the kite in the half of the power zone on the side you are traveling) or point the board slightly downwind to build up some power if the board is a bit reluctant to get moving.

Turning in the opposite direction means that you will have your back to your kite and will be riding with pressure on your toes rather than your heels. Before you try a complete toe-side turn, first practice riding on your toe side on a hill, without the kite. Once confident enough to try a turn, start pointing the kite upward toward the zenith while pressuring your toes. You are aiming to make a wide, sweeping arc with your board. By maintaining pressure on your toes you will bring the board all the way around to face the opposite direction, where you need to dip the kite back into the power zone on the side of the direction you are now facing. You should be able to lock the kite into position in your new direction. Try to keep the board moving steadily throughout the turn, as stopping midway will give you problems.

To turn back again so that you are riding on your heel side, apply the same rules as above but pressure your heels rather than your toes.

How to get air It is not recommended for anyone to try to jump with a board on – certainly not without having had the benefit of some instruction. If you do attempt it, wear protective gear.

Concerning the movements of the kite alone, jumping with a board is achieved in much the same way as jumping without a board: having built up resistance, fly the kite in the opposite direction or simply upward toward the zenith. You now need to consider the taking off and landing of your board. If you can, practice jumping with your board on minus the kite (it looks a bit silly, as you will get only a little bit of air, but it will help you when you are trying to deal with so many new skills at once on your first few jumps). You need to be very flexed at the knees leading up to the jump and to keep your weight centered over both of your feet. At the moment you want to jump, push up and slightly backward, pulling your knees up toward your chest as you do so. When you come to land, flex at the knees and ankles to absorb the shock of the landing.

For more air time, send the kite back in the opposite direction the moment you are airborne. This also ensures that your kite does not stall or luff when you are in the air.

Snow-kiting/kite skiing/snowboarding

Kite skiing is used as a generic term referring to both snowboarding and skiing with a kite, but, confusingly, it is occasionally also used to refer to kite waterskiing. A simple description of snow-kiting is adding a kite to snow skiing or boarding, enabling you to ski/board on flat terrain as well as up and down hills. This sport has gained popularity in cold climates: for one thing, it is a fantastic alternative to paying exorbitant lift prices to get up mountains, and for another, it eliminates the necessity for skis or snowshoes to get across flat areas.

Equipment

The tricky thing about snow-kiting is finding appropriate terrain, rather than finding the right kite to use. As snow is in fact just frozen water, many kiters use water-relaunchable kites on snow, but it makes more sense to use a land kite. Land kites are easier to set up and pack away; they become lifeless pieces of material when depowered, so they are arguably less of a threat in a tricky situation; and they do not have inflatable bladders that may split if the kite crashes to the ground. If you choose to use a land kite, it should be of similar size to one you would use for landboarding – if anything, slightly smaller. If you choose to use an inflatable kite, you would use a slightly bigger kite than if it were a foil, because "tubes" do not generate as much power as foils – but not as big as one you would use for kitesurfing, as you need less power to pull you on snow than in water. As a rough guide, a 145-lb. (65 kg) beginner

in force 3 should be happy with about a 25-ft. (8 m) inflatable kite. Foils tend to offer more power for their size, whereas inflatable kites tend to generate more upward lift.

It is a matter of personal preference whether you choose to use a bar or handles to control your kite, but for beginners a bar is generally less of a problem, as you can fly it with one hand while you deal with putting on/taking off your board. You are also able to lock it into position while riding, which you are unable to do with handles.

Kite skiing and kite snowboarding are pretty similar but both have their idiosyncrasies. Boards (assuming they are bi-directional, or "twin-tips") allow for easy tacking as you do not have to turn around to go in the opposite direction; you simply go backward ("fakie" or "switch"). However, once you do turn around, riding on your toe edge isn't as comfortable as on your heel edge, as the kite is flying almost behind you. On skis you have the advantage of increased mobility when the need arises to walk, but the disadvantage of having to turn fully each time you tack.

Whether you choose a board or skis, for snow-kiting they should be relatively short (about up to your chin when placed upright) and flexible so that you can cope with varied terrain. Asking for a free-ride ski/board – a board designed for varied terrain – will get you the right setup. The average ski with its quick-release bindings is more suited to snow-kiting than the average board, which has strapped bindings, making it impossible to release the board from your feet in a hurry. If possible, choose a board with step-in bindings if you are boarding. There is also the possibility of using blades – very short "trick" skis – if the terrain is pretty smooth.

Whatever you choose to ride on, make sure the edges are razor-sharp to grip the snow so that you can create good resistance to the pull of your kite. You may also want to use a seat or waist harness if you are experienced, as well as all the appropriate safety gear – helmet, impact pads/ shorts, gloves, map, compass, etc.

Basic skills

Many people find snow-kiting a less daunting alternative to kitesurfing. First, a kite pulling you on snow does not need to be as large as one to lift you out of water. Second, you won't sink as you would do in water if you have teething troubles with your kite (as long as you are not riding in powder). This makes life a lot easier when you are getting everything ready for takeoff.

As for all kite sports, make sure you are proficient in all the relevant skills before you start. This means either skiing or boarding, as well as kite flying. Those who partake in skijoring (being pulled on skis, employing the bare minimum of control, behind a galloping horse or a vehicle) should be able to jump right in.

How to set yourself up If you have a friend to help you, ideally launch the kite and have him or her hold it while you put on your board/skis. Otherwise, put the kite into position on the ground, then get your skis/board on and face at an angle of about 60° from downwind. If you are on a board, sit down with the heel edge digging into the snow and your knees bent up to your chest. Launch the kite, digging in the edges of your skis/board that are farthest away from the kite to prevent yourself from being dragged downwind.

How to get moving When you are ready, dip the kite into the power zone in the direction you want to travel. Once you decrease the edge angle of your skis/board you will start to slide. You may have to fly some sine waves to build up power, but ultimately you want to maintain a steady position of the kite in the air at about 45° from the ground. It is important to fully utilize the edges of your board/skis. If you do not lean away from the kite, dropping your knees toward the ground on skis, or digging your heels in and leaning back if you are on a board, you will not be able to prevent the kite from pulling you downwind. You are also likely to catch an edge if you let your skis/board lie flat, which will result in a fall.

How to stop Slow your momentum by flying the kite gently upward toward the zenith while turning your skis/board upwind away from the kite. Stopping suddenly requires fine-tuning the synchrony of these two skills, using a more assertive turn away from the kite (a parallel or skidded stop on your skis/board).

Maneuvers

How to turn For boarders, the idea is exactly the same as for landboarding, in the section above. You can choose either not to turn the board but ride fakie/switch, or to turn the nose of the board 180° and change from riding on your heel edge to your toe edge. To ride switch, lift the kite to the zenith until your board comes to a stop, then lower the kite into the other side of the power zone. The board will then start moving in the opposite direction. To turn the board to face it in the opposite direction, again fly the kite upward toward the zenith, but this time slowly rock your weight forward over your knees as well as forward toward the nose of the board. Your kite should be nearing the zenith, but do not hover it there or it will stop your momentum. You are aiming to keep the board moving all the way through your wide, sweeping arc-shaped turn. By applying pressure to your toes halfway through the turn, you will bring the board all the way around to face the opposite direction, when you need to dip the kite back into the power zone on the side of the direction you are now facing.

As for turning on skis, you do not really have two options (you could ride switch for novelty value but it's slightly on the pointless side of productive – unless you are about to take off and spin some big air trick). So, fly the kite upward toward the zenith. As the line tension begins to ease slightly, allow the edge angle of your skis to decrease and bring your weight over both your skis. Start pointing your skis downwind, beginning to pressure the opposite ski to bring you around into a sweeping arc-shaped turn. As you complete the second part of your C-shaped turn, lower the kite into the power zone in the new direction you are traveling.

Riding on steep terrain Like snow to a puppy, it's all a bit confusing when you sprinkle in some variable gradient to the flying/riding equation. For example, often the zenith will be far behind your head rather than above you, where it is usually, or you may find yourself battling against the kite to move forward, while trying to ride downhill. The trick is not to look down. Be aware of imminent changes in the fall line (the hill may slope off to the side, rather than straight down) and be ready to adjust your edge

pressure to compensate, but do not keep looking down. Keep an eye on your kite when you can, and certainly keep your line of sight up at head height, letting your feet feel what is going on below you. More often than not you will try to look down and apply what your conscious mind thinks your body should be doing. Your balance is much better off when controlled by your sense of feel, along with your muscle memory, leaving your sight to control your direction.

Once you are confident on varied terrain, you will have little trouble pulling off some small tricks using the fall line and the kite, and eventually getting big air (if that's what you are looking for) by using the kite in the same way as you would for kite landboarding, buggying or surfing.

Getting air This is achieved in the same way as for all other sports in terms of the kite's positioning. When the terrain offers you something to jump off – a lip or a kicker – you will need to fly the kite upward to prevent its pulling you too laterally rather than vertically. Make sure that you put your skis or board flat when taking off and landing to prevent throwing yourself off balance, and flex your knees on landing.

Water-based traction sports

Kiteboarding/kitesurfing

Although there are different ways of using a kite on water (for example, kite kayaking and kite waterskiing), kitesurfing (or kiteboarding) is the most popular and well known of all the traction kite sports, and perhaps the one to thank for the speedy development of all the others. It was interest in kitesurfing from the windsurfing community that helped push the sport from the obscure into the mainstream and encouraged the financing of research into equipment. It is also one of the trickiest sports to get the hang of, as the water adds another complication to the flyer-kite-wind equation.

Whatever you choose to play with on the water, make sure you really understand your kite and its emergency release system before you go out on the water. You will need a bigger kite on water than you would on land in the same wind, so this is an added reason to make sure you are confident of your skills.

Kitesurfing is just like windsurfing, with a kite instead of a sail, or like wakeboarding with a kite instead of a boat/cable. It is surfing with a kite and can be done either in waves or on the flat, as long as there is wind! Standing on a wakeboard/surfboard hybrid, you let the kite pull you back and forth across the wind.

Equipment

It is imperative that you use a four-line kite for safety, and a much better idea than using a two-line, as you have more chance of keeping the kite exactly where you want it in the wind window. As a rough guide, a beginner of 145 lb. (65 kg) should be happy with a 33-ft. (10 m) kite in force 3 winds.

You will want to use a bar rather than handles to control the kite so that you can use one hand to put on your board, swim back to a board you have left behind, or style out some air with a grab. You will also want to use a harness (when you are proficient enough to do so), as you will be dealing with strong winds and big kites and your arms will get tired.

It is a good idea to start with a big board in light wind, as it will be more stable and buoyant, meaning the kite won't need to generate as much power to keep you afloat. A good setup for a beginner or improving kitesurfer would be a twin-directional thick and wide board that, when placed on its end, reaches about roughly to your shoulders. The length is important, but width and thickness are more so. If a board is wide and thick, it will pop up easily and feel stable and keep going if the kite depowers. Do not be tempted to start out on a board with a thin profile, as the lack of buoyancy will not do you any favors. As you progress, you may want to change to a thinner board – with a narrow waist for going fast or a wide waist for freestyle.

Your board will have fins attached to its base to help you direct the board. Bigger fins with a thicker profile will help you stay in a straight line, which will save much frustration when trying to get upwind. Make sure that the foot straps on the top of your board fit you well so that your feet don't swim around, causing you to lose some control. Beginners should choose foot straps that allow you to release your feet quickly; wakeboard-type boots will cause you trouble if a large kite is demanding your attention while you spend 10 minutes trying to get your board off.

Opinion is divided on the subject of leashes. Although it is a miserable experience trying to swim upwind to pick up your escaped board, it is less miserable than being knocked out by your board as the leash snaps it back toward you when you crash. If you wear a leash, do it with the knowledge that it is dangerous, and always wear a helmet!

NB If the wind is strong, use a smaller kite and board. If the wind is weak, use a bigger kite and board. Make small adjustments by changing the angle of attack (see page 15) of your kite.

Basic skills

In all kite sports the wind is the first thing to consider. For beginner kitesurfers this is even more important, for both the wind speed and the wind direction dictate whether you can take to the water or not. This is because, in most instances, the shoreline will be running from top to bottom in a standard direction. Beginner kitesurfers ideally need the wind direction to be cross-on or cross-shore, or, at worst, cross-off. If the wind is offshore it is inadvisable to surf unless you have a backup boat.

There is an extra step when learning to kitesurf that other kite sports do not have. Between learning to fly the kite and kitesurfing you must learn to fly – and relaunch – the kite in the water without the board. Flying in the water is called body dragging and is much the same idea as scudding on land.

Body dragging Before you learn to kitesurf, or indeed on days when the wind is too weak or gusty to kitesurf, you can take a shot at the macabre-sounding body dragging. Body dragging happens whenever you take to the water with your kite but without your board, letting the power generated by the kite drag your body through the water. The fun of body dragging is trying to get your whole body out of the water as you pass the kite through the power zone. The not-so-much-fun part is walking your kite back to where you started! A further advantage of learning how to body drag upwind is that you will be able to retrieve your board when kitesurfing if it is left upwind of you after a crash.

Launch your inflatable water kite as usual, at the edge of the window. Hover the kite at the zenith, or lower, at the edge of the window, if there is a chance of lofting. Walk your kite to the water until you are submerged to just below chest height. From this position, start dipping the kite into the power zone using figure eights. On each occasion, dip the kite a bit further into the zone, and allow it to pull you, in a Superman pose, forward and up out of the water.

How to set yourself up Once you can fly the kite with one hand, are a confident body dragger, can relaunch the kite in water, and can use the kite's power to lift you up from a sitting position on land (a dry water start), it is time to pick up your board and walk into the water. Just as for walking when body dragging, keep your kite either at the zenith, or lower down, at the edge of the window. In the water, hover the kite above you, sit down so that you are bobbing in the water, and place your board in front of you, heel side nearest to you. While keeping an eye on your kite, put your feet in the straps so that your knees are bent up near your chest and the board is sitting on its edge in the water.

How to get moving

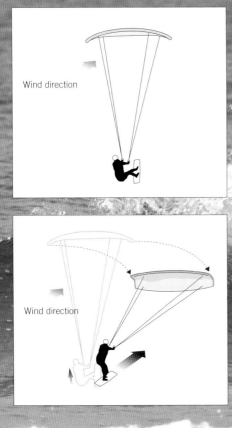

Wind direction

Wind direction

How to get moving When you are balanced, fly the kite firmly into the power zone on the side of the direction you wish to travel. The power generated should lift you up and out of the water. You will need to keep your weight on your back foot to keep the nose of the board out of the water, and lean back onto your heel edge. Keeping yourself from sinking is your immediate concern, so pay attention to your kite and keep it moving through the power zone in figure eights until you have enough speed and poise to lock the kite into position at around a 45° angle from the water.

How to stop Turn your kite upward slowly toward the zenith. At the zenith your kite will stop generating power and you will slow down and sink.

How to stop

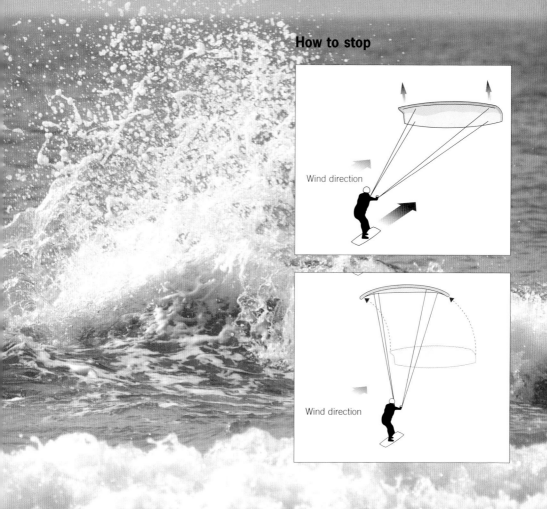

Wind direction

Wind direction

Maneuvers

Getting upwind is tricky, both on your board and off. The first time you will probably need to do this is when you have crashed and your board is bobbing around upwind of you (if you are not wearing a leash). You will need to fly your kite high near the zenith in figure eights, while putting an outstretched arm in the water in the direction you are being dragged, but pointing slightly behind you. Eventually you will be dragged upwind.

Surfing upwind is more difficult than windsurfing, and, of course, a problem that wakeboarders do not encounter. Whereas a windsurfer only has to trim the sail and steer the board, a kitesurfer often has to really work the kite and the board. At least it is not necessary to turn the board's nose 180° to go back across the wind if a bidirectional board is used. With twin-tipped boards, just as for landboarding and snowboarding, you simply raise the kite to the zenith and reposition it on the other side of the window, allowing you to ride in the opposite direction with the opposite foot leading. To gain ground upwind, make sure you keep the kite powered up, high and close to the edge of the window, and cut as far upwind as you can with your board, using your head – if you turn your head to look upwind, you will invariably travel upwind.

How to turn To turn the nose of the board 180° you will apply the same principles that you would on a snowboard or landboard, as above, taking extra care to keep the kite sufficiently powered up – sinking in the middle of a turn is irritating, to say

the least. If you are not using full-foot bindings you can change your footing in mid-turn so that you are always riding on your heel edge with the same foot leading, or, if your feet are fastened down, you will ride on your toe edge.

How to get air The same principles apply for getting air with a kite on a board as without a board. If you are traveling to the right, send the kite left and upward toward the zenith while at the same time doing a sharp right turn on your board, away from the kite. This should lift you. Instantly send the kite back right again so that you can land and won't get dragged backward. You can use waves to give you more air, executing your sharp back-turn on their crest. This will mean you do not need so much backward movement of your kite to get as much air.

5 Safety

Safety is a huge issue in the fast-paced sport of power kiting, and important even if you are out flying a single-line kite. Injuries really are avoidable if the simple rules outlined in this chapter are followed. Make sure that you read this section before you take out any kind of kite. In many areas kite flying is restricted for safety reasons, so check out the regulations where you are. If you are kiting on a beach you should find notices on the beach itself outlining what is and is not permitted there.

Safety guidelines

The following tips are intended to outline some of the most important aspects of safety connected with kiting. Wherever you take your kite and whatever kind of kiting you intend to do, always exercise caution and use common sense.

Choose an appropriate site

▷ Give yourself as much room as possible downwind of the kite.
▷ Make sure there are no obstacles behind you, such as high buildings or trees, as these will disrupt the wind and cause unpredictable gusts.
▷ Power lines ANYWHERE in the vicinity are life-threatening.
▷ Do not fly near airports, roads, pathways or railroad lines. Use common sense for other areas. Be aware that kites scare animals more than humans.
▷ Warn those around you where you intend to fly.
▷ Make sure you are authorized to fly in that area (check with the local authorities, who should have designated fly zones and no-fly zones).

Choose appropriate conditions

▷ Check the wind conditions and choose a kite appropriate for the wind.
▷ Check the tides if you are off to the beach to fly, and pay attention to any warning flags that may forbid you to go in the water.

▷ If the wind is too strong choose something else to do.
▷ Always launch at the edge of the wind window.
▷ Never go out as a beginner in a strong wind. Learn in lighter winds.
▷ Don't let a beginner fly your kite in a strong wind.
▷ Never fly in a storm.
▷ Try not to fly alone.

Choose appropriate equipment

▷ Check your equipment for wear and tear; don't fly with equipment that needs mending or replacing.
▷ Always wear safety gear – especially for buggying, surfing, boarding and other high-speed sports.
▷ Make sure you have a working quick-release system if you attach yourself to your kite.
▷ Make sure your equipment is suitable for the wind strength and your experience.
▷ Make sure your lines are appropriate for your sport – that they have sufficient breaking strain for the kite(s) you are flying and that they are not too abrasive. Kevlar is too abrasive for flying in close proximity to others, for example, when buggy racing.
▷ Don't forget to pick up your stake if using one.

Protective gear

Even though you can minimize the risk to yourself by using common sense when flying a kite, it is a good idea in recreational kiting to wear some protective clothing. It is essential if you intend to add to the equation any hard materials such as a board or buggy, as these hurt if your head is thrown against them when your kite suddenly gets the better of you. Investment in the following is highly advised:

Helmet – lightweight, inexpensive and a real lifesaver if your kiteboard pings back on its leash and hits you on the head.

Knee and elbow pads and other body armor for land-based traction kiting.

Gloves are a good idea to prevent callused-hand syndrome, and are also useful as protection against lines that can cause bad cuts.

Flotation aid/impact vest for water-based traction kiting.

Warm and waterproof ski/board clothing for snow-kiting.

Sunblock – even when it's cloudy.

Long-sleeved tops and long pants cover your skin to prevent any abrasive action if your kite does get the better of you and drags you across land.

Don't forget to empty your pockets – landing on a bunch of keys hurts!

Insurance

Third-party insurance is a must for traction kiting in case anything does go wrong. Even if you are the most safety-conscious flier, you can still be surprised by random joggers appearing out of nowhere with energetic dogs who love to chase moving objects. The easiest way to go about getting the right insurance is to register with a national body such as the AKA (American Kitefliers Association) or CKF–FCCV (Canadian Kite Federation–Fédération Canadienne du Cerf-Volant), or to join a group such as a buggy club. Many designated kite zones will not allow you to fly power kites unless you have third-party insurance.

Fitness and strength

Insurance companies will cover you financially after accidents have happened. This is important. Arguably more important is making sure you are fit enough to take part in the first place. While most single-line kite flying requires the minimum in terms of strength and fitness, some stunt kiting and all power kiting demand that you have a reasonable degree of strength, fitness and coordination. Make sure you can hold on to the kite you have chosen should a gust pick it up. Don't consume alcohol before kite flying. Make sure you can swim well in open water if you are kitesurfing. Make sure you have warmed up your muscles, as you will undoubtedly use parts of your body that have been lying dormant for a while.

Children can take part in flying kites and all the related kite sports, because you can easily adapt the size of the kite to suit their size and strength. However, sending your six-year-old out into raging waters with a kite and a board may be a bit over the top. Children under seven will find it hard to hold on to even small power kites and to employ the coordination needed for most power kite sports, but they can still fly single-line and stunt kites. This is not to say that under-sevens should be excluded from kite sports, as there are certainly exceptions.

Just apply some common sense and recognize that kite flying is a sport and not simply a walk in the park.

Glossary

Airfoil A structure that provides lift when in motion.

AR (aspect ratio) The wingspan (length) divided by the chord (width). A kite with a high AR will have a wide wingspan and short chord.

Beaufort scale Scale invented by Admiral Sir Francis Beaufort to quantify wind speeds.

Body dragging Being pulled through the water by a kite, without a board.

Catching an edge When the edge of a board/ski that is leading in the direction of travel drops low enough to the ground/water to catch and halts forward momentum.

Chicken loop Quick-release safety feature on a control bar attached to a harness. When you pull it, you detach yourself from the kite.

Delta kite A kite with triangular wings.

Diurnal variation Diurnal means daily. The variation describes the relationship between the sun and wind speed. High sun = high wind speed. When the sun drops, so does the wind.

Fakie Riding backward on a board/skis.

Figure eight Imaginary 8 shape created by flying a kite back and forth across the sky.

Flysurfing Kitesurfing.

Foil Short for parafoil – a land-based kite that gains its shape from the wind filling its cells.

Freestyle Tricks.

Getting air Using the kite to get airborne.

Infinity Horizontal figure eight.

Inflatable Fixed-form kite with inflatable bladders, used on water.

Jibing Turning your board around to face the opposite direction.

Jones, Andrew British pioneer of modern ram-air kite design (1970s).

Keel Triangular fitting on some kites that aids stability.

Kite ground-boarding Another term for kite landboarding.

Kite kayaking Being pulled in a kayak by a kite.

Kite landboarding Being pulled on land on a skateboard hybrid by a kite.

Kite skiing Being pulled on snow on skis by a kite.

Kiteboarding Usually refers to kitesurfing, although some use the term for kite landboarding.

Kitesurfing Being pulled on water on a surfboard/wakeboard or hybrid by a kite.

Lark's-head knot A knot used to attach kite lines to the kite.

Lofting When the flier is (involuntarily) lifted into the air by the kite.

Luff stall When the kite loses power suddenly.

Lynn, Peter New Zealand pioneer of kite buggying in the 1980s. Probably the first person to customize a three-wheel buggy for kite buggying steered by the feet.

Merry, Ray British pioneer of modern ram-air kite design (1970s).

Moonwalking Kite jumping, when the kite is used to lift the flier.

Ollie A certain type of jump evolved from skateboarding where the nose of the board rises first but the board lands flat.

Parafoil Non-rigid kite, also called ram-air, where the wind inflates the canopy.

Popping ollies Jumping.

Powell, Peter British pioneer of modern stunt kite design (1970s).

Power window The difference between the minimum power a kite can generate and its maximum power.

Power zone The area in the wind window where the kite is more directly in contact with the wind, generating the most power (the kite's wind profile is largest in the power zone).

Ram-air Also referred to as a parafoil, a non-rigid kite that is inflated by the wind (parachute + airfoil = parafoil).

Sheeting in/out Adjusting the kite so that it harnesses more of the wind's power or spills it.

Skijoring Sport where you are pulled on skis/board behind a galloping horse or a vehicle.

Snow-kiting Being pulled on snow by a kite on a snowboard or skis.

Spar A strong bar used to give structure to a kite.

Spreader bar Metal bar on the front of a harness to which the kite is connected.

Stall Luff; when the kite loses power suddenly.

Surface area – actual Physical surface area of the kite.

Surface area – projected The surface area that faces the wind when flying.

Switch Riding backwards on a board/skis (riding fakie).

Tack As in sailing, the direction a wind-powered vessel travels in.

Tacking Changing direction by turning your vessel downwind.

Trucks The fittings that attach wheels to the base of a board.

Tube Inflatable kite.

Twin-tip Bidirectional, two-nosed board.

Wind envelope Wind window.

Wind window The area downwind of a kite flier in which the kite can be flown. If the kite is flown outside this window it will stall.

Wing loading Weight of a kite divided by area – the lower the wing loading the easier it is to get the kite airborne.

Zenith Center of the top of the wind window.

Index

Acknowledgments

Thanks to Grandpa, Mum, Dad and Ginny, Jonathan and Harry Cobb, Kate Mitchell, Sam Geek Bourton, Little Laura Wake (HTP), Jim Collis, Tony (www.kiteboardacademy.com), Victoria Alers-Hankey, Serena Docker, Duncan Craig, Blake Roseveare, Henry Hallward, Janie Airey, James Butterfill, Richy Stones, Dreya Wharry, Justin Pugh (www.extremekiteshop.com), Vic (www.sky-fly.com), Jigger, Ben Jackson and Oli (www.londonbeachstore.co.uk), Jeremy Pilkington and Matt Ferris (Flexifoil).

Thanks to Watergate Bay for providing the location. Go to www.extremeacademy.co.uk for more information.